DON'T SEARCH, CELEBRATE!

THE COLLECTED POEMS
OF MANSUR JOHNSON

MANSUR JOHNSON

Other Titles by Mansur Johnson

Murshid: A Personal Memoir of Life with American Sufi Samuel L. Lewis
Available on Amazon and in 99 libraries world-wide

Shamcher: A Memoir of Bryn Boerse and His Struggle to Introduce Ocean Energy to the United States
Available free on line or for download at www.mansurjohnson.com

Letters from Moineddin
Available free at www.mansurjohnson.com

Big Tales: All the Stories in the 12 volumes of the Sufi Message of Hazrat Inayat Khan, by Hazrat Inayat Khan, Compiled and Edited by Mansur Johnson
Available on Amazon

COMING SOON

In the Footsteps of Alexander the Great

The Bowl of Saki Life of Samuel L. Lewis

Travels with Marianne

Mutu Kubla Anta Mutu, Die before Death

DON'T SEARCH, CELEBRATE!

THE COLLECTED POEMS
OF MANSUR JOHNSON

MANSUR JOHNSON

Published by The Einstein Academy
Tucson, Arizona, USA
2017

Published by The Einstein Academy
Tucson, Arizona, USA
www.mansurjohnson.com

Author photo by Sharif Munawwir
Interior Design and Cover by Jelaluddin Hauke Sturm,
www.designconsort.de

ISBN 10: 1540773760
ISBN 13: 978-1540773760
Library of Congress Control Number: 2017900552
CreateSpace Independent Publishing Platform
North Charleston, South Carolina

Dedication to Moineddin Jablonski

Moineddin is the contemplative guy on the left of the author, who faces the camera, in the cover photo. We met at a bar where he worked called Li'l Bill's in Iowa City, Iowa, at the University of Iowa near where the photo was taken. I'd recently arrived to obtain a PhD, following my academic mentor from the University of Illinois, where I'd completed a Master's degree before going to Mexico. In Mexico, I took LSD, and I had to hitchhike back to Champaign, Illinois, from San Antonio, Texas. After spending a week in jail, someone decided to deport me, as a *persona non grata*, from Mexico, for cavorting naked during that acid trip, some of which is portrayed in the poem "Ithaca" in the collection below, entitled "Don't Search, Celebrate!", which are poems from the psychedelic 60s.

My one acid trip in Mexico with Thad and Rita Ashby, who were colleagues of Timothy Leary and Richard Alpert, gave me an experience of mysticism. "All is one," say the mystics. Thad and Rita taught that LSD is a sacrament, and I agreed. They are represented in the poem "Ithaca" as "a man" and "woman beautiful." (See "Ithaca," Part IV.) I returned to academia at the University of Iowa in Iowa City wanting more. More of what? More acid! More mystical experiences!

To that end, I purchased from a chemical company enough ergotamine tartrate for about 10 million doses of LSD. Sound like a lot? Remember LSD is measured in micrograms. Our friend Kurt knew a chemist in Chicago. The chemist failed, however, to produce any LSD, but instead concocted psilocybin, a type of psychedelic derived from mushrooms. "Magic mushrooms" became our mystical vehicle.

Moineddin was a poet. I am grateful he appreciated my poems. But I disagree with his reframing of this book's title, *Don't Search, Celebrate!* (See Author's Introduction) That title came to me as a realization. Lord Buddha said, "I see now all people are enlightened; they just don't realize it." The perception that "All is one" is a deep realization which should, I believe, be celebrated, no matter how one obtains this realization.

Moineddin and his wife and, soon afterward, my wife and I, joined the hippies in San Francisco and discovered the man, Sufi Ahmed Chisti, Rev. He Kwang, Zen Master, Samuel L. Lewis, who became our teacher. Sufi Sam, as he became known, recognized Moineddin, who had an uncanny resemblance to his teacher, Hazrat Inayat Khan, as his Khalif and successor. And for 30 years (1971-2001) Moineddin held the post, until his untimely death due to complications of kidney disease. Rest in Peace, dear friend. Thank you for your friendship.

Mansur Johnson
December, 2016
Tucson, Arizona,
USA

CONTENTS

Introduction by Mansur Johnson

Moineddin Jablonski inspired the publication of *Don't Search, Celebrate! The Collected Poems of Mansur Johnson*. Here's how. In a 1984 letter to Allaudin William Mathieu, Moineddin wrote:

> I recall fond memories of Mansur Johnson, speaking of drawing together the loose ends of our many journeys, exiles, prodigalities, what have you. Back in the mid-sixties, he wrote some prodigious acid poems, i.e. "Blue Monday," "Ithaca," and others. They were all gathered under the title DON'T SEARCH, CELEBRATE!
>
> As intoxicating as this dictum was to us "realized" acid heads, the sobriety of Muhammad's "We have not known Thee as Thou shouldst be known" has proven to be a maturer view.
>
> Therefore, let us now CELEBRATE THE SEARCH!
>
> —From page 220 in *Illuminating the Shadow: The life, love and laughter of a 20th century Sufi, Moineddin Jablonski*, Edited by Neil Douglas-Klotz, Sufi Ruhaniat International, San Francisco, 2016.

+++

How could I resist Moineddin's inducement to publish? But wait, DON'T SEARCH, CELEBRATE! is only 43 pages of psychedelic poems from the 1960s. That's too small a book to publish. And if it isn't well received? I'll never publish more poems. What about the rest of my poems? Life is short. Why not offer all of them? OK.

You have in your hand: *Don't Search, Celebrate! The Collected Poems of Mansur Johnson*, 280 pages.

"Delicious!" raved Najat Roberts, Moineddin's former secretary.

Thank you, Najat.

LIST OF POEMS

DON'T SEARCH, CELEBRATE! (1964)   19

SACRED AND PROFANE POETRY
(1969-70)

Poems from *MUTU KUBLA ANTA MUTU, Die before Death (1974)* 127

JOURNAL POEMS (1976)   145

THE HEART IS AN OCEAN
from MURSHID (2006)   *255*

THIS IS IT
(To the Present, 2016)   *259*

DON'T SEARCH, CELEBRATE! (1964)

Blue Monday

Let me tell you a movie bout a film I know.
It's partly a dream and a kind of peep show.
The characters are almost all the same,
Although they don't go by just one name.
You could for sure distinguish at least two,
But, if they put on clothes again, the stew
Of naked bodies playing on the green
Has suddenly with slow dreaming gestures
Put between what they seem
A thin blue layer the mystery
Cinematic purity cannot clean.

Stay high
Get by
Don't fly
To the sky
Cops see
The pot tree
Drug scene
Evergreen
LSD
Inside of me
No where to go
Take a boat
It won't float
Around the world
No girl
Is a pearl
With me
Or anywhere
Always wants
Her share
Can't pare
Fingernails
Green snails
Clam juice
Redwood spruce
New York

With a fork
No where
To go.

I am social.
I am alone.
I am happy.
What is that?

I couldn't bare it
To share it,
Your love, Ruth darling,
With some other it.

Take a guy (an asshole virgin)
And give him his best friend's cock up his ass.
See how one gives his love so willingly
O daughters of Jerusalem, love thy neighbor.

I love the church as myself,
At night extending ex tapestry,
Gesticulating for Jesus Squirt.
O ripeness desires death as perfection uptown.

But would you commit adultery if I read your poetry?
Mark three windows with black
Pencil five hot plates on back
With *Marca Registrada* Mexico D.F.,
Pronounced day effy in the Spanish alphabet.

Liz takes the act for all,
Plugging guys off the streets,
Showing off her juicy treats,
Saying once again what she repeats,

Luck out.
Way out.
Get out.
Can't,
Can you?

Silverstein has abruptions,
An erupt ending, snake eaten,
For get it, or never mind, not
Like *Hiroshima Mon Amour*.

Shel is still very young,
Only 39, two years less than Weldon Kees
(1914-1955) when he died,
And knows it's not getting across to be hip;
Good moments, too bad, without eternity.

A *Playboy* photographer dropping tips right and left
Waited for weeks to get a hold of 007 on the beach,
So that he could take him for his magazine,
In an exclusive column coming: Way Out of Thunderball.

We all listen to Bobby Dylan and try to copy him,
And that whore who wears street walking boots on the cover,
And that too svelte, slinky, black-haired sophisticate,
Blasé bobbysocker, probably without any morals in him.

But heroes uncovered, Bach bounce
Drug up, read the magazines and be everywhere at once
Except where you are
Boxed.

Corn like nobody can
Music that just makes you feel grand
Them's the 20s and Barry Goldwater today.

I don't work at it,
Or I'd be good.
And I don't work at it,
And it turns out good.
Analyze that.

All this talk about niggers is social stuff.
Who hangs with a nigger that doesn't work,
Meet, party, treat, buy, play, write, sell, compete, repeat.
All this talk about niggers is social stuff.

More work and less play will keep the niggers away,
The man say,
What makes you pay,
Shoots with a sting ray, rap-pety rap, rap a long way.
The scholar man is master of the past,
Studies stuff the scholars of that last
Day didn't know themselves, especially
Everything the bards were singing.

Up to date anthologies—new,
New, latest stuff, movement, publication, thing, hip, fad,
Far out,
Unanachronistic present daily newspaper,

Not for Albert Schweitzer *Teufel Himmel*
Who abolished time for timeless misery
Martyrdom, in the jungle, away from civilanity.
I wonder, if he's happy, what is that?
Just a passing comment on the scene
Makes me a commentator without spleen.
To be more clever and lose my clean
Would require a more diligent than passing scene.

See, when I was young I used to think
That institute rewarded brilliant think.
And so with ink and tongue and pen,
I continue to fail and then

All my ambition out from under me goes,
Down lower, deeper, more problematic than my toes.
What was it doing down there at all?
When it should be most clearly on the wall.

Like my diploma and all the riches that situation brings,
A PhD maneuvers skillfully on college teams.
An audience, status, X-KE to drive
The babes home on cocksure situation status thrives.

Let me tell you bout the levels, groups of colony,
The magazine world, film, movie, cinema, Bobby Dylan too.

And the newest one of all is the university
With lots of guys refuging there like me and you.

Like a big vacation with all the other folks away
And all the time a myth, a making music cross the line,
Crying, college! the new line. And if you're big enough,
You and your like make it all the time.

The scene going on in the next room,
Multiple booms (for the film's sound man)
And records playing TV sounds,
While the desert Riff song of Gordon MacRae
Plays while John Wayne is chasing something at sea ...

What's this? A new drink?
Which serves instead of capsule sugar for the tea
LSD, and room sounds.

It's all vibrating! The whole room
Is trembling as a heart beats on the loom
Of our skilled artificer's bloom,
Which pierces deep into your womb.
But tell me, What value is a present participle rhyme
O piercing with some assonal agreement
Sticking, pricking, for example?

El valor 50%,
But don't forget the rent.
The rest is the epilogue of licking,
Bringing up to 90
The incongruent additive
Piercing, present participial farcing.

And O boy now
Bring it round,
The happy joyous plow sound.
O what? O what?
Is what we want to know.
What's that?

A cat meow! On the make
Muzzling up to fat fruit cake;
Takes his paw into her pouch,
Bites her neck and gives her ouch.

Without a sound, sex round:
Lick a tip and bite a ball.
All for give and take a fall,
Circle round, eternity bound.

Flesh, skin, ape, shin, mayflower thin,
Get you gone without my rod,
If you don't have the nicest bod,
God's harpoon will get your sin.

Monday morning, Monday morning,
And my head is bad. And my head is bad,
But it's been worth it. Oh yes, worth it,
For the time I've had on Blue Monday, sad.

A Small Frosted and Ornamented Cake Cut

Where am I going to live?
How am I going to get the bucks?
Too many tos,
Petit-fours confuse
Blue dream beat ice cream.

Niki

I don't care.
It don't even matter
Whom you are
Wakening with
Tomorrow,
As long
As you are
With me,
All day
Today,
Everyday.

Ouch!

When you say stop,
"Stop! Please, too much,"
I hesitate to say
It's just the beginning
Of the "pain" you will feel
At my joy and your expense
Of pleasure.

Hey, You'd Better Hide Your Love Away

Hey, Carl Jablonski in town now at Bill's,
There's a CIA man in here now on pills.

He's a head! A lawman, badge-bearer, red Communist
In town now at Bill's, there's a man going to bust us.

Us?
Communist!

Stop folks. It's alright, cause Chap has just said,
The pusher and dealer and officer too
Are not here today, so go back to bed.

It's Bigger than Both of Us

We've got a club,
My love and I,
And freedom and independence
Are dues
We extract from each other,
And others,
All of whom we want,

Except those two girls
And that man, who courts my love,
Cannot come with us just now,
(Although I seem to contradict myself).

It's just that
Those two girls
Want me to be to them
What I am with her.
And just now I only have time
For those who are both of us.
That's you and Pat and Carl too.

The Same Generation

By someone from the Silent Generation

- iGen, Gen Z or Centennials: Born 1996 and later.
- Millennials or Gen Y: Born 1977 to 1995.
- Generation X: Born 1965 to 1976.
- Baby Boomers: Born 1946 to 1964.
- Traditionalists or Silent Generation: Born 1945 and before.

www.genhq.com/faq-info-about-generations

Every once in a while
Sing it now, sing it loud
It is good to give a name
To what is. Gertrude Stein, I
Suppose, began it all.
When? Why when
She pointed out the Lost Generation to Hemingway.
Since then, beside Lost, we've seen the Jazz,
Beat, Jive, and God knows how many other generations.
I now propose the Same.

The *O nobly born*
Same Generation
Is for life, as opposed
To death. But to clear
The austere air of contrary angry confusion,
It is necessary to state that they are,
Or can be, one. *We die each moment* or other similar
Clichés successfully captures the mood I try to describe.

Not surprisingly
The nobly born
Young instigated this
Wonderful madness,
Which cries crystal tears
For revolution at Berkeley and
Sucks a sugar cube in Harvard Square.

Yes, and if there were a war cry, it might go
Sing it now
"We want everyone
Except those
Who don't—*sing it now,*
Once more time now, bring it round—
Who don't want us."

Like Hamilton Camp
From his album *Both Sides of the River*
The Same Generation sings,
"Love is but a song we sing;
Fear's the way we die.
C'mon all you people now,
Let's all get together and
Love one another right now."

The Same Generation is Ginsberg talking guru talk,
And Norman Mailer digging President Kennedy, and pasting LBJ
Upside down everywhere, in order to topple his usurpation
In 8 years. Everyone in the Same Generation knows God is
Mao and Lyndon too. The CIA man in Li'l Bill's in Iowa City,
The CIA in our mail and bugging our telephones
Is the Gestapo to everyone in the Same Generation,
Because Bobby Dylan, not Dylan Thomas, sings it now,
One more time, all together now.

Wow! This line of thought
Is an uncontrollable
Reaction to the *Time*
Magazine Sunday Supplement
Establishment whose interesting
Dull dimwit prose is, yes, aggravating.

Clearly contemporary culture is revealed
In magazine *Modern Living* dissection zoology 101,
While keeping with fashion and fad, mode and
Taste, in and out, and current social, intellectual, and
Sporting jet set members, our mighty journalistic organs seem
To avoid, even in analytical reasoning,

A basic contagion: pleasure.

The need to get with something new leads to something else new,
Parody recapitulates originality and becomes it, part
Of the continuing effort everywhere, but
Perhaps factories of all kinds,
To vanquish, *O soft now*, boredom.

A traditional song sung by someone new, is something new,
And an old hand repeating traditional songs is
Probably pleasing himself, if not you.
If not, perhaps he changes or adds film to song like the Beatles.
Rarely is change exclusion.
It is development, addition, and
All the folk-niks who turned
Against the beat-niks
When Bob Dylan sang folk rock
Probably don't deserve to be niks.

And what *Playboy's* well-dressed and undressed sex is trying to do for
The body politic and its clothing, SPIDER in Berkeley (representing Sex
Politics International Drugs Extremism and Repetition),
Tries for the Same Generation.
Playboy, of course, is part of the establishment, but
It is Same Generation establishment,
Because it speaks well
About so many things.

Sonny and Cher's green suede vests, for example,
And pop art shirts are not unrelated to
The well-pressed *Playboy* image. We
Can arrive at pleasure many ways,
Consider clothes a costume and
Move, sing, walk, stream of
Consciousness through
Role, act, play, game, and
You've got pleasure.

Playboy, your excellence is characteristic of the best of the Same Generation.
A recent *Des Moines Register Sunday Supplement* notes

How Roger Vadim is out of the cultural jet set now,
Because his recent films have been of poor quality.
Note how jet set sniffs are not insensitive to box office,
And I would argue that artistic
Excellence does not exclude financial success,
Point out how every good artist has made money,
In spite of the fact that
He's sometimes dead before the world finds him.
That's the Kafka story.
It's unfortunate but frequently fact
How some art world pedants enjoy arguing,
Is Walter Keane's art in good taste?
Is Walter not oblivious to this sort
Of talk as a member of the Same
(*You too, my friend, can come if you sing*) Generation,
Telling *Life*, "They pick on me because
I'm out here,
Not in there."
O boy such
Pedantry must,
However, be
Acceptable
To the Same Generation,
As long as the talker
Likes what he's doing.

Remember the Protest.
Remember?
Remember how members of the Same Generation protest?
I don't recall seeing that.

But we must assume shortcomings sapped their archetypical
Figure Tim Leary who smiles serenely upon everything, like Buddha,
Or Nureyev, and we know there are
Some members in jail.
Ken Kesey is there for blowing pot.
Sometimes the next generation's prophets
Are the last's criminals.
Kesey's supposed to have said
Something like, "I've given up

35

Writing for awhile. There's
An infinity of time needs
To be spent inside jails
And riding buses."

Perhaps the Same Generation is an old religion,
A syllogism or some clichés:
Christmas is everyday,
Put the X back in Xmas.
Ever hear of Xtian ethics?
Me first reversed.
Whatever.
Its sickness is the divine comedy contagion
Of laughter 007 style.
Its esotericism is pleasure,
And its apocrypha is work.
All the Same,
But there's a lot of babble always
About members of this Generation trying to escape
Reality. Here today it is important
To remember
To mention that everyone there
(In this Generation)
Would categorically reject any
Classification.
Education is the only answer
For babbling or stuttering;
Hence, it is fruitless
To say that reality is
Well, out with it,
Sing it loud,
Reality is what gives.
            +
"Now that I understand death,
I'm awfully busy dying life,"
Said an old black man,
Watching the river go by.

Glue and Breen Fearform Search Smell

I don't like to read D.H. Lawrence,
Mann for more than 28 pages,
Modern poetry,
But I'll see your novel if it's made into a movie.

I don't rank Joyce for very wrong,
But stand him longest as the best since him.
The medium of personality makes art stride on.
Today they're telling stories which stink of unconscious parody,
Smell without a myth or cult which it gestalt,
An organized whole that is perceived as more than the sum of its
parts.

Preaching blood is negative.
Great form per se is too blasé.

The Germans made the music, the French look at Phenomenon.
("Our program of musical literature thinks," thought the smiling
blond soprano in her chair playing *Israel in Egypt* somewhere. It's by
the German Handel.)

The USAs are trying hard.
The hope is education,
Education, education,
"It sounds like a train,"
Choo-choo-hoo-boo
Choo-boo-hoo-choo
Choo-choo-hoo-boo.

O where is personality and art?
The Beats were vital once a time.
The Pops are coming off the line,
And words have gone besmirched.
Poets academic
Make their circles for their stuff.
The movies folks are here.

Elizabethan theatre meant audiences.

And then the 18th century,
A restoration of the stage,
Supplanted by the novel beast,
5 volumes full of letters,
Neat and tidy secret lives,
Now bound and all into the 19th century.
But first, Dickens never seeing
Wordsworth, Blake and Keats, Shelley, Coleridge
The mind a ridge,
The vision Alps,
The message far.
The truth just here.
Forgotten.

Tarnished thought-fed Blake
Saw iron dream toil in Yeats,
While Jimmy Joyce
Stayed home
To lay ole Molly turdsweet womansblood
ALLWOMB EARTHUGE MANURGE DREAMSHEN FINNEGAN.

That's it—but don't repeat, "this is it," Zen lovers.
Find ole Mary Moran and
If you want to make some art
Try a movie with a tart.
And remember,

I don't like to leer
(*Leer* is Spanish for *lire*).
Smart ass, that's French for
Something we don't do much here,
Less pass psychedelic cheer.

Why is It Lonely Traveling Alone?

There is a story in Homer.
I didn't read it in Homer,
But somebody else read
Homer and said what he said:

How in the beginning
Man had four arms and four legs,
But then there was the division,
And man split apart.

There are thousands of books which write
About the subsequent imperfection
(Taking her hand) but I want
To be concerned with the perfection.

In my art, we shall travel.
I confess, I love what caresses me.

Alright Stand Up and Be Drafted

Alright!
Raise your right hands and answer loud and clear:
Who's for America?

We are ... America the beautiful ...
Spacious skies and
Amber waves of grain
And purple mountain majesties
Above the fruited plain ...

Alright!
Who's an enemy of the state?

We are ... communists and queers.
We just love liberty, Constitution, Bill of Rights,
Everybody, like the Bible says
Even addicts
We just love to be intoxicated ...

Alright!
Probably use narcotics too.
Do you?

A B C Z
Let's see,
A narcotic soothes pain.
A narcotic induces sleep.
A narcotic distorts reality.

PROTEST MARCH

Is probably used by doctors only
To soothe, induce, or distort
Painful cancer reality
Enough to permit patient pleasant death.

PROBABLY DON'T APPRECIATE WHAT THEY'VE GOT ...

Alright!
Son, ...

NOR APPRECIATE WHAT WE'VE GOT TO DO TO KEEP IT

What?

You keep going like this, and you're going to find yourself
In deep water ...

Over my head?

Out of sight, prison doors, a thing of beauty, wilting forever,
Tasting the ashes, tasting death in his draft card ashes ...

What color is Brahms?

Alright!

Nazi Germany ... democracy ... freedom ... rights and privileges for feel
And think and love

AMERICA!

Land of purple
Mountain majesty,
Amber waves of grain,
To protest
Detest
Molest ourselves
And Santa Clause on a one horse open ...
Family. Families that slay together stay ...

ALRIGHT!
All right,
Alright. Oh
Help me sonny
Son!
Sun
To stay at home

And love my son
Who's been drafted.

Wish Upon a Star

Have you ever tried to swallow an ounce of pot,
When the cops ask you, "Hey you! What it's all about?"
Have you ever tried to swallow an ounce of pot?
Because that 28 grams is a lot of pot.

Say you're walking around the campus with a small bag of pot
To the tune of *Have you ever wished upon a star?*
Have you ever carried moon beams home in a jar?
Have you ever wished that you are
Something more than you are?

A roach holder in a talisman cult,
Lucy in the sky with diamonds is code;
Moses is a Catholic, and
President Johnson
Attends baptism.
California prices, Acapulco gold quality Mexican,
Repetition becomes duration. Oh

Have you ever tried to swallow an ounce of pot,
When the cops ask you, "Hey you! What it's all about?"
Have you ever tried to swallow an ounce of pot?
Because that 28 grams is a lot of pot.

There's the time I sang to the President,
"I'm writing clever songs, sir, rather than spew lies to please the
people."

Even still, there are some people who say I can't sing,
But I sing everything since Wagner's Ring.
I sing from the pulpit, the baldachins, those
Ceremonial canopies of stone,
Metal, or fabric over an altar,
Throne, or doorway, from the steeple and the hills.

I sing so much— I believe exposure kills—
About the people and the words that they use.
And all the time I'm singing my song,

There's a House Committee asking me my views.
Have you ever tried to swallow an ounce of pot,
When the cops ask you, "Hey you! What's it all about?"
Have you ever tried to swallow an ounce of pot?
Because that 28 grams is a lot of pot.

I say, "Sir, I'm a lover, a communist, but I know that word's no good,
Cause the communists, they're our enemy, and we're for everything good.
We're for peace and resurrection, Jesus & the cross, the army's
Round the White House, while the niggers mind the boss."

He say, "Niggers, you're the people that has all the fun,
But first of all present yourself and, here, take my gun.
Go into the foreign countries, where the resurrections come
And kill them dirty communists, who ruin all our fun—
And steal their country's resources, our profits—what a pun!"

Have you ever tried to swallow an ounce of pot,
When the cops ask you, "Hey you! What's all about?"
Have you ever tried to swallow an ounce of pot?
Because that 28 grams is a lot of pot.

Where's the prophet? Why
They're the communists with ideology
For to win the hearts of men.
His arms were swinging now like dual windmills
In ecstasy. Pretend
That there is nothing else.

Utopia is no place, that's for sure.
It's *ou topos* in Greek, where words are pure.
And now, we're in Greece, and it's time to split,
And lamps around here everywhere are lit. Oh,

Have you ever tried to swallow an ounce of pot,
When the cops ask you, "Hey you! What's it all about?"
Have you ever tried to swallow an ounce of pot?
Because that 28 grams is a lot of pot.

Mama Lament Circle Song

Once when I was a child
I could tell the difference
Between butter and margarine,
Real orange juice and frozen,
But my mother told me it was impossible.

Then I began to do
The kind of kidding the next generation
Barely understands was risqué.
A liar and a storyteller,
Making things seem true,
All things seem true that are false.
"Seem" means to be perceived and

All things can be perceived, for example,
"Only your eyes know," mingles vision and knowledge.
This is all true so far, but note:
Nothing about understanding has been mentioned.

One does not understand, one knows,
And by knowing understands that he cannot know.
It must follow then
That he understands.

The past is undichotomous assertion, a unity.
It speaks of androgynous chthonic rites, polymorphously perverse,
An immigrant god who slays the god of music,
Just as discotheque dooms the city sympathy,
But not today.

Today, the Technicolor movie called life—
C'mon in, the water's fine!
How interesting those man machines are! And the sounds!
Mingle altogether *insieme* in Italian
Einanander wander *junto* together in Spanish
Alone, seeing that a role is important for then
Game structure is established.
Once my mother wondered why we couldn't be friends,

So I'm going to take my projector home and turn it on
And let her see the same world she probably knows about
Already, because she's been telling me
For years to get married, ever since she broke up
Jeanne and me. In fact, she doesn't understand.

Dear Mother

The reason you were never satisfied, never happy
With me, for not doing anything for the house,
The yard, the basement, or the attic, for never doing anything
For anybody, especially you, is

Well, the reason I never did anything for the house,
The yard, the basement, or the attic,
Never doing anything for anybody, especially you, is
I had no guidance from you.

You never did anything for me,
Except bear me and, remember,
I cried then too.
Please forgive me, I exaggerate.

You have your theories and traditions,
Appetites and sorrows, goals and roles, ambitions and reconciliations
To what might be, and isn't, and all that might
Have fraught your mind when it was young and pure.

Had you remembered, you might have seen,
That the way of children is the way of their friends, and
Elders can be that, if they're still surprised
With love that marries what it cannot do without, or rejoices
With tragedy that twists a troubled mind into satisfaction.

But what? Oh what? O mother sun does
A son do with a mother who cannot pierce, for heaven's
Sake, the cotton candy ditch which suffocates the son,
Who suffered loss with the first tear
And found the world when he combed her hair,
The hair, mother moon, of my mother earth wife.

Note from the Underground

I once knew a girl
Who thought herself queer,
And on public occasions
Tried to make them all leer.

She saw Mary, Mary,
A girl misunderstood.
Her fantasy world
Was where she stood.

The idea of people
As screwy as she
Would preclude the movie
And force her to be.

She delighted, in fact,
Yes! Her only game
Was to seem a freak;
Hence, loony, but tame.

One thing was clear
She was smart as a tart
To befuddle the masses
Her primary art.

Yet second to this
And comforting too
Was her love for a fellow
We all know as Pooh.

Wednesday's a day
But also her doll,
If only her hero
Was more like a Moll.

This poem is not angry
Spiteful or droll,
Rather written by someone

Something like a mole.

I said I once knew her.
In truth I still do.
If that world is false,
I'll surely be blue,

For moles are a strange breed,
Blind and alone,
Lost underground,
Light-hearted they roam,

Self-pitying
Two-legged
Rascal
Egg

Fox.
I am
Going now
Into the box.

Dance and Sing and Dream in Front

The human instrument is
The most beautiful instrument
In the field of music,
So let it dance,
If it can.

It can't, unless its energy is unquenchable.
Energy without sleep that seems unquenchable
Must dance, but
If I dream all day long,
Do I have to dream at night?

They say that dreams are
Healthy, wish-fulfillment,
Expiatory, consolidating
Catharsis, and I believe it,
Because I feel so fine,

Since so long ago.
How many centuries
Have beaten back at the sun,
Since I stopped wishing at night,
For what I've got all day long?

Behind closed lids, behind closed lips,
Everything is the same,
Sometimes black, sometimes bitter,
Sometimes dreamy,
At night behind closed lids.

It is black, but
Automatically f-stop eyes open, eye
Balls roll, back and down,
Everything out of sight.

Things are seen
With huge black eyes,
Dream like unrepressed,

Sometimes
Bitter,
Sometimes in blinding color,
Everything never quite the same,
Behind closed lids, behind closed lips.

Makes the Music Stop

Stop is a word which marks a spot
Which isn't necessarily the top,
But it's got "top"
In it.

Something like anger
In the sign danger DANGER,
Which you don't always see in time,
Or know where it is.

Yet when stop becomes a spot
Like make a book
Of poetry,

Publisher, letters, frontispiece, artist's abstract
On the cover, index, title, numbers maybe
On the pages, words, of course, and all the ink,
And binding movie rights, and copy cats,
And everything that makes a book,
But nothing ... shit,
Read the title,
Makes the music stop.

Our Town

Yes, there was a man in our town,
Who invented the supercharged finger.
'Twas on the Benton Street Bridge
One evening in early winter.
The ground was wet
With dew and melted snow,
And three ducks were ...

"Is it still today"
"What day is today?"

The perception of the bourgeoisie that there exists a difference
in time and rhythm between their lives and ours marks a real
advancement in the obtainment of a pure democratic order.

"You said that already."
"I did not."
"Yes, you did."
"I said it just now."
"No, you said it before."
"What did I say before, 'bourgeoisie,' the word bourgeoisie?"
"No," (giggling) the whole thing.
"You mean the perception of the bourgeoisie that it is a very
dangerous thing to be driving along and to be passed on a scooter
by a moto going 60 miles an hour, when there exists a difference in
time and rhythm between ducks and humankind, which don't swim
in icy rivers?
"Yes."

Non Poem

I couple, you couple, he couples, we couple, you couple, they couple, and, of course, it couples. Hast-du vergessen eines auseinandersetzung? (i.e. Have you forgotten an exclamation?)

"We're both going in opposite directions, so I think I'll go for a bicycle ride," go for a bicycle ride over to see a friend. "I wanted you so much," I'll say tomorrow to my friend who isn't home. "O friend, dear love, why aren't you home? I want you so much right now." There's a naked woman home somewhere right now!

What's worse for a man to love another man or another man's wife?

Bread and milk, popcorn and a Skyrocket, orange sherbet in a paper sleeve, Coke and two hotdogs and a beer, three Pepsis, hard-boiled egg, liverwurst sandwich and milk, sweet pickles, tomato and lettuce, vinegar—all the necessary elements: vegetable, vegetable, vegetable, meat, milk, egg, bread, of course, scrambled eggs and hash browns.

Have you ever seen a couple walk in the street or, for that matter, lie down in the street?

Fight,
Party,
Flee,
Search,

Confusion, anguish on top of a high rise, with balconies which go around the top is, well, 3 dimensional thinking (if you can see it that way), profound, insightful, perceptive, or something.

My favorite poet is Anais Nin. My favorite fiction writer is Anais Nin. My favorite language is lingua Maya. My favorite time is no time. Here we are.

Get Along

When you think your *yoni* gets dry,
And my *lingam* starts to die,
When thoughtless it is quite hard.
Forget the wise words of the bard:
That since the dampness of the flood,
Earthlings possess short-lived blood.

Did you misunderstand my written mark,
Not wanting to enjoy a lark
With present and with future bark?

Friday was in a different condition, after all
My intellectual curiosity fulfilled too, without a ball,
Although I still suspect that possibly my paints are on your wall.

I wonder what,
"I suppose I've put my foot in my mouth
In my normal fashion especially with males," means?

There is no time in paradise,
Babe, and Milton didn't write it.
And speaking of the bark above, which *Paradise Lost*
Itself as I imagined paradise? I am
Going visiting tomorrow ... going to go
Swimming ... going to go watch ... it's going to be a good show that
I'm going to ...
Wish you were near.

Near here, *no where,*
U topos, in Greek.
Nothing need be transformed
Into cornucopia if you are here.

Measure of Displeasure

The problem today is not mortality, nor morality;
It is vitality.

Beware of catch phrases, but do not shun life,
Life that only unfettered inactivity can rear.

Let the love of living interfere with everything
Else less important.

Encourage your neighbors to enjoy a session.
Witness the energy of excellent delight always without measure.

And never exude displeasure. No.
Nein (pronounced 9) in German, never,
It is contagious.

The tenth confinement, without amendment, nor commandment, craves contentment,
And that's all.

Masturbation Necessary

No idea why
Just that I want to.
And want to
Is what is,
Which is more important
Than why.

I am pleased with nothing
Being written today.
I intend always
To be a spectator,
Neither smiling nor pitying,
Cold and hard as life itself.

The contradiction is immediately visible, as I mention my belief in
endless development, in equidistant directions, without value, in the
preoccupations of human kind.

Accompanying this development is
The capacity to burn out.
New art forms recur as surely as fads:

Hula hoops, Frisbees, skate boards, the Beatles, Elvis Presley,
Stop the Music, President Kennedy, Dada, Pop, Op Art, Steiger
and TV, black and white; buck, blue suede, saddle shoes; cowboy,
army, desert boots; pink and black argyle socks, French cuff links,
ascots, cummerbunds, and Levis at Fire Island, Newport Beach,
Sausalito, Lake Leman, Puerto Darios, Saint-Tropez, Iowa City; Paul
Engle, Patrice Lumumba, Moreau, Marcello, Bunuel, Mario Savio;
millionaires, multiversity, escalation of federal aid, teach-in, college
campus, 8 and ½, *Playboy*, Buchenwald, Mauldin, Herblock, Norton
Simon!

Here in today's time, there is
A magazine world which admires our war time
President and his uncommon passion for
Accumulating great wealth,
More money than any individual could spend in many lifetimes.

The $50,000 it takes to be frozen at death until "the cure" is found
Explains neurotic society, but not
Five thousand additional billionaires.

Poem Originally Written in the Shape of a Tree

All round the forest, there were the cottages, and all round the cottages, there was the sea, and all round the sea, there was the sky, and all round the sky, there was the earth, and all round the earth, there was the forest, and all round the forest, there were the cottages.

You are in a cottage, all around the sea, around the sky, around the earth, around the forest, around the cottage, where you are in.

You feel comfortable because the cottage is all around you.

Everything is flat as you look around you, and every thing around you is not you, because you are not flat, unless I see you, but I cannot see you now.

I can see you now, and you are flat.

I am not flat, because I am not you.

But now I am not in the cottage.

There is no cottage.

There is nothing but the sea and the sky.

There is a fire in the forest, and you are in the cottage.

The cottage is green, and you are laughing, because all round the forest, there were the cottages, and all round the cottages, there was the sea, and all round the sea, there was the sky, and all round the sky, there was the earth, and all round the earth, there was the forest, and all round the forest, there are flames, and the woman next to you is caressing you.

If you could find your hand, you would caress her too.

But your hands are busy now, typing this poem.

Shreela

Thinking about the mysterious death
Of the Asian woman,
As two businessmen spoke
Of sober speculations on the possibilities,

I knew instantly that they knew
Of her death. So did the man approaching.
They know everything in small towns.
And what was her life to the world?

To a very small world, sorrow.
To the rest of us?
Nothing. The crowd is full of puppets,
Bouncing skeletons,

Doing a death dance, waiting for void,
Vibrating and spidering,
Hither, thither, down the street.

The day was grey and bright,
Transfigured, dusty day time,
Waiting for death, walking.

Impatience

That high note
Someone sings,
I can't do it.

Alone,
I'm always ...
That why I need you.

Our union is unequal,
But do not judge yet.
I do not know what it means.

I would ask you as a virgin:
Are you a deer, a mare, or an elephant?
Am I a hare, a bull, or a horse?

The possibilities of interpolation are vast.
I cannot presume
Without anyone to ask.

I know already, see,
You are an elephant—
Grotesque as it seems—
And I, lo, a bull.

So the question I began with
In my mind, seeing you with him:
Is he a horse?

Even before that, I thought of the vastness
Of a bull with an elephant.
I am so full, I thought.

How fine to be swallowed
In unequal union with an elephant,
Who prances like a doe or even a mare.

But it is clear why she is with him, a horse.

What good is a bull who thinks like a horse,
If he's not with her?

To my Teacher, Kurt Vonnegut, Jr., Why I Can't Read Anymore

A joke is a display of humour in which words are used within a specific and well-defined narrative structure to make people laugh. It takes the form of a story, usually with dialogue, and ends in a punch line. en.wikipedia.org

It's not because I read slow,
Although I do.
You see, it's the words
Which make me go
Along swinging with the rhythm
Mood and song,
In even the most prosaic
Dull dimwit book of prose.

But to get to the books,
And why I don't read much anymore,
I'll have to say, just
Out with it like fact,
Or truth,
My view anyway,
"They're all just, well, a sustained **joke**
And who's got all the time in the world
Right now?"

Middle Class

The author is a genius ...

No, let's see
Which vocabulary am I using?
I mean to whom am I speaking?

Er, ah ... I can speak any language, and
Language and its usage is characteristic, you know,
So let's see,
What does genius mean to the reader?
Who is the reader?

Ticket-seller, which is code for an ordinary person.

To him? He's a smart man, different and perhaps
Eccentric to the middle class.
To her? She's a smart woman, different and perhaps
Eccentric to the middle class.
They look away, or straight ahead, pretending they
Don't see his costume,
They look away, or straight ahead, pretending they
Don't see her costume,
While those that laugh are out of sight,
Sometimes laughing with you, sometimes in jealousy, or
Self-amusement, don't know why,
Unconscious maybe,
They don't try
To be confused,
It's simply that for what they're used.

Ithaca

I.

Common experience of pure sensation.
Careful integration of mind and body,
A fusion of both
Before an unsuspected possible.

This harks from uncommon
Employment which throws man over willing into alienation,
Perhaps adding to it with a Brandenburg 3,
Or intoxication under the sun on a May Day early afternoon.

I'm tired of critical allegories.
Parodies?
Each week someone tells us how unhappy death-wish Herman
Melville was
How black, how pessimistic, how skeptical of his pessimism ...
What else is there but allegory to eat?
Would you please cut that word?
Rarely can I dismiss words, though inclined to silence,
I am reminded that it is death.
Well done sir.
Rock back forth, between do and don't, in and out, closed open box ...
Voices braised and skewered, Filipino anagoge.
The only alternative?
Yes, eternal yes, smile summer snow, while winter blow
Us toward

II.

A place called Ithaca,
Where one day I was reading
In great repose, although my mind
Was racing and enjoying. In
Front of me
Were Leopold and Stephen,
Taking cocoa, and the author
Was the interlocutor.

It was greatly mental business,
Getting into their minds
Through the *recit*, when it dawned on me:
The two were one
In the mind of the author on the page.
The style was close.
There was no information
About one as distinctly opposed
To the other. They
Had always seemed two, but no,
And the author was mad, but author still,
Only suggesting to me that
Life is imaging two for one. The keys to—given!
A way, a lone, a loved, a long, the knowledge
Being stated a priori
By an exemplary delusion of mind. But
There it was, the secret of life,
And no one ever told me that before
In that way—That is poetry, if I can use
A weak word for the rage I felt
At those who wouldn't tell me it,
And they were teaching it!

III.

Do my words seem febrile to you?
Then see, nothing can be said,
Except another anecdote
About the trick, this time the trick
Of life, which can be introduced
By analogy to the club
Which is very hard to join, the
Fraternity of scholars, who
First go active (degree wise) then
Pledge their school until vacuation
Doth them part.
                Pretend now you are
Taking the examination.
The community of scholars sits out there.
Their aggregate of courses on the page

Of our fair handbook lurks imposingly
Behind their combined stare—sinister glare.

I wanted to vouch forth a suggestion,
Not too rash, that we about to answer
Might have knowledge and a man together
Against we match our researches—who is he?
And whence he learned? With whom he studied and
How much he earned, the first year free like we
Soon hope to be?
                    Visionary power
A proposition from a viewless mind,
The guild grants thee not the power of their kind.
Begone now dream for they are questioning me.

And when you finish answering, they say NO!
After you come back into the room,
All are standing, with fire shooting out of their eyes,
Some waving weapons, pens and forks,
While they reject you and send you
To a niche, where you not knowing all your
Comrades have theirs too, until the
End when all have been condemned and
You are sent to the great damp hall.
Looking with shame at those who won,
You think, until it is announced:
All have passed, all have won, and you are now
One of us. You won, but you thought
You lost, and now with victory
So strongly accented, you don't
Know what? But this as introduction
Is sufficient lead in to the story:

IV.

There was a man who was a strong
Influence on another, when
One day the other found himself
In another world, which was the
Same one transfigured, vibrating,

Timeless, beautiful, form-full of
Yes, and "a man," old and young in one middle-aged man,
And "woman beautiful," the words
He, this another, used to describe
The young lady he desired.

During the moment of high confusion in Paradise,
He asked his companions to please
Tell him the story of the man
Who influenced him so—"Tirel,
Tirel," he shouted.
"Who is Tirel?"

Tirel, good friend, said the
Noble Roman passing the jug of wine to his mate, *Tirel is*
One of us. He's in on it. He's
No stranger like the withered breast
Or the ranting robots outside of us,
For we are inside the center
You sought, and he is one of us,
Although absent.

And thus I learned my influence
Was in on all the trick, part of
The journey to some East, but
Forbidden to speak of his importance,
Save through others while absent. Now
It is known. The joke is
Manifest jokeness, and I see
The trick that was. Needless to say,
How relieved of burdens of thought
I was at the knowing. And now,
I am living still, and I still
Remember the great discovery
I made about the influence
I rarely see anymore. And

Something to my mind then was
A joke, and then what was, was perfect.
But then is not now, nor I doubt

Was it then, because shortly
After I learned about the trick
Of my influence and sublimated
The desire I felt and went off
To find the light, I
Lost all consciousness of what was,
Wandering naked on the grass,
Screaming in tongues I barely knew,
Until I saw the light in a portal behind the wall and, lo,
My friends in Paradise were there,
Opposite, in the building there
Bounded by the steel fence which
Was nothing—I ran right through it,
Just like in a dream. I even
Gripped my teeth for the crash which did
Not, never came—I ran through it,
And I embraced my comrades until
It ended suddenly. I go
No farther for a blow on my
Head ended this there, only to
Return in a dream hours past,
Layering the difficulties.
Until now, I search the onion
For the form to tell this strange
Supernatural tale. And

V.

I choose Melville's moral: We must have
Confidence, which is probably
Comedy, faith, the strength to try
The holy land and live, called what
You call it. Life is an allegory any
Way for appearance how you see
It. Let there be life to relate
Books somehow: super transmerged
Natural intoxication
Until death, which is what the Bible
Says, and at the end of confidence,
Which is more important?

The extinguished light, the darkness,
Or the man leading the man off?
Or the man leading? or the man?
Or the—cosmic joke—temporality
Of it all?

It could not be extinction, because
They are walking after what, when
Light goes out, is called death.
Extinction, resurrection,
It is help and, like Freud says, the
Reverse, not leading, being led
Into light. No truth intended
Here, only embodiment,
Original, saintly,
Contradictory, subsuming, a real,
Comedy. The curtain drops at the first
Snicker, with reversals in infinite
Regress, forward,
Two ins make an out,
A life a death,
Someone said.
Eli Eli lama sabachthani?
My God, My God, why have you forsaken Me?

SACRED AND PROFANE
POETRY
(1969-70)

Driving through the Desert alone at Night

Dear Murshid,
How do I know when you come?
When I feel a chill of bliss
My friend
I know you have arrived.

Is not communion open
With all the saints?
Yes, all that is
Necessary is concentration.

What great art is worth
The memory of any living mortal?

One that is remembered with devotion
With joy
With admiration
With respect
With desire to emulate.

The life is hard
All have shown it,
But MOHAMMAD,
Ah, Mohammed.
Ramadrishna did not appreciate you.

What one has to go
Through before he
Turns to God!

When I smoke cigarettes, I lose inspiration.
I lose inspiration because my passages become blocked.

Ah, it is too simple.
Inspiration.
God is the breath!

By watching my breath

I learn to consider
Every situation independently.

Like watching to see what element predominates
By feeling rather than by consulting memory or the time piece.
Delete space

So much being written.
What of lasting value?

What of lasting value?
The effort of a man to learn about himself
And thus to learn about others.

My mission, my dharma, my duty—
Many who have grown up think about their mission, their dharma, their
duty.
Knowing human nature, one feels it must be demonstrated.
It must be exemplified in my own self.

The inspiration comes and works of art can be made.
The master brings it at will.

The Passionate Nymph to the Shepherd

(Angrily) You had time to fuck
me but you don't
have time to talk.

THE SHEPHERD'S REPLY TO THE NYMPH

You weren't fucking me?

Untitled

Does
It
Bother
You
That
Someone
Can crawl
Right
Inside
Your
Head?

Memory

Get in the mood
And deliver the message
You had
Dressed in a certain costume
At that particular time
When you called me,
O my beloved.

Kermit, the Hermit Saint of Novato

Dedicated to Van

The hermit saint of Novato
Lives in the water-meter well.
"You'll be known as the 'Saint of Novato,'
I told him, "if you keep acting so swell."
You see people give the saint diseases
They cannot get rid of, like
One lady who came by with whooping cough
She'd had for twenty years,
And another had scarlet fever
She'd had amidst her first born tears.
He took them all with cold and flu
And moved out of the well
And lives with only a sleeping bag
And one umbrella still.
And thus I named him, "Hermit,"
To go with, "The Saint of Novato."
But folks here still call him, "Kermit,"
And don't make too much bravado.

Love

Love is putting out the cats
When you know the old lady
Doesn't want them
In the house.

Zen Flesh, Zen Bones 1

The Sir Francis Drake cutoff into San Anselmo Avenue in Fairfax.

The one thing I don't like about America is the stop sign.

Zen Flesh, Zen Bones 2

Everything has an emotional feeling.
When you can see that feeling,
THEN!

The freeway north of San Raphael at rush hour,
A photograph titled
"The Mass Migration away from the City."

Mrs. Frisch's Garden

I worked for eight hours in Mrs. Frisch's garden.
She is Spanish and Mr. Frisch is German.

I worked for eight hours in Mrs. Frisch's garden,
Pulling grass out of a small patch of dichondra.

I worked for eight hours in Mrs. Frisch's garden
With only two trips to the bathroom,

And for practically the whole time,
Mr. and Mrs. Frisch worked in another part of the garden,

Kneeling close together
Lowly speaking her language.

"Life is beautiful in Spanish,"
I thought.

Ten Sufi Thoughts
by Hazrat Inayat Khan

1. There is one God, the Eternal, the Only Being, none else exists save He.
2. There is one Master, the Guiding Spirit of all souls, Who constantly leads his followers towards the Light.
3. There is one Holy Book, the sacred manuscript of Nature, the only scripture which can enlighten the reader.
4. There is one Religion, the unswerving progress in the right direction towards the Ideal, which fulfills the life's purpose of every soul.
5. There is one Law, the Law of Reciprocity, which can be observed by a selfless conscience together with a sense of awakened justice.
6. There is one Brotherhood, the human brotherhood, which unites the children of earth indiscriminately in the Fatherhood of God.
7. There is one Moral Principle, the love which springs forth from self-denial and blooms in deeds of beneficence.
8. There is one object of Praise, the beauty which uplifts the heart of its worshiper through all aspects from the seen to the unseen.
9. There is one Truth, the true knowledge of our being within and without, which is the essence of all Wisdom.
10. There is one Path, the annihilation of the false ego in the real, which raises the mortal to Immortality and in which resides all perfection.

The Objects of the Sufi Movement, by Hazrat Inayat Khan

1. To realize and spread the knowledge of unity, the religion of love and wisdom, so that the bias of faiths and beliefs may of itself fall away, the human heart may overflow with love, and all hatred caused by distinctions and differences may be rooted out.
2. To discover the light and power latent in man, the secret of all religion, the power of mysticism, and the essence of philosophy, without interfering with customs or belief.
3. To help to bring the world's two opposite poles, East and West, closer together by the interchange of thought and ideals, that the Universal Brotherhood may form of itself, and man may see with man beyond the narrow national and racial boundaries.

The Poet Gives a Poem to the Infant Nuria
b. October 30th as a Present

Scorpio born beauty, in February
I knew you'd been conceived. To say
I fathered you would be a lewd confession
Worthy of hoary Zeus himself, but what reticence
To tell a tiny she-babe: I met your mother in a dream
And spilled my seed in bed like cream.
This is my Aquarian dream mystery child,
I give you roses of passionate dream.

Kamasutra Sutra

Breath is a very important element in lovemaking.
The consciousness of the breath of one's Beloved
Is essential in the union of two who would be Lovers.

+

Caresses must originate with the out breath of the caresser.
To be properly received caresses must be
Given to correspond with the in breath of the Beloved,
Who must be treated as none other than your own self in these matters of
Love which would be successful.
The moist vulva or dripping member must be taken as a sign of success in
the matter of Caress.

+

Kisses should carry with them the force of the whole being.
They should be entirely spontaneous, treating the lips as vehicles of the
Holy Spirit,
And the breath containing thoughts of Love deposited anywhere on the
body to be among the most sensual of acts associated with the expression of
Love known in India as Dharma.

+

EXPOSITION OF THE GENERALIZATION THAT VARIATION IS THE
ESSENCE OF LIFE AND HENCE LOVE

As we enjoy variety in life, so
Variety in Love is of the spice.

+

When separating from a woman or wife,
Speak about passionate times with her in the past,
Ask to make love many times during the day.
Determine the exact time when your hearts were first united,
Offer to help her move,

Tell her you can see her move will be for her a rebirth of freedom and joy,
That you can see her laughing and jumping for joy over her new found freedom and strength,
Tell her that you see that her move will be for her an awakening into new worlds of freedom and soul unfoldment, where she feels free as a bird.

Road Kill

Higher speeds are tolerated here,
Not the lower ones.
I got a ticket for going too slow
On the freeway.

Paranoia

Being stopped
An officer
Searches and discovers
A bag of pot
On this person.

Sura, A Chapter, or Section of the Qur'an

Say, I love you.

My Love

My love plays the guitar,
And I do Spanish dances.
She says, "Pick up your feet."
I never miss a beat.

We drink wine together,
Hold each other tight.
She tells me a story—
I turn out the light—

Bout the time together
We lived long ago,
Read each other poetry,
Watched the river flow.

We have known each other,
Since I saved her life.
She was good to me,
Acted like my wife.

We have known each other,
As long as songs were sung.
I have been a singer;
She has played a drum.

I was once a pirate,
She a lady fair.
I knocked off her old man,
Began to stroke her hair.

She didn't recognize me,
As fast as I'd have liked.
It took a few more centuries
Before I did it right.

You see, she's always played guitar.
I've always been a dancer.
Her music's been the melody
That makes all hearts beat faster.

Passing through the Mind While Sitting in Child's Restaurant Looking Out at Boston Commons

"This town is too unpretentious to be Boston."

My Prayer

Dear God,
Please make your nest in my head.

Trans World Airlines: London to New York

I like to eat
Because it makes my heart beat.

He Lit a Cigarette in the Seat Right in Front of Me on the Bus

Millions of marvelous buildings
Throughout the world
Have installed tobacco air conditioners.

April, 1970

Reading Walt Whitman
Is like riding on a bus
Through London
To the airport
To New York.

One Morning on Novato Boulevard

A schoolboy stopped on his bicycle,
Looking for something with his hands in his pockets.
With that look on his face,
You know his mind's in his hands.

Catherine, a Woman Poet, who Used to Drink

You loved a man,
A child I am told.
He wrote some verses
And your heart unrolled—

But now you've grown up
And laid your glasses down;
Your face is smiling now,
You've buried your life-long frown.

The Merry-Go-Round

If a woman leaves a man for you,
She'll leave you for another too.

Free Advice

"Don't get," he said,
"What you can't keep near bed,"
With half his love, half his hoard,
Under the bedroom floor board.

Last Rites

The dying Old Man
Who reaches up
To squeeze the hand
Of the Old Nurse
Knows that the Sorrow
Of one human being
Is the Sorrow
Of the whole world.

Aphorism

Anybody can lift up our love from us,
Like chicken from a bowl.

Last Wednesday

Last Wednesday, I fell in love with a man.
Before, I'd only seen his beard and nose.
Last Wednesday, I saw his eyes and what it shows:
Love's in those eyes I fell in without clothes.

A Question

Tell me,
Is
Your mind
At
The end
Of
Your eyes?

Lost

I am lost in a line drawing of eyelashes.

Dialogue

The Knight asked:
What is noble, what is love, and what is won by winning?

The Preacher answered:
The deep desire of the heart is not won by sinning.

Divorce 1

The saddest words
Written up on the wall
Are, "I guess I didn't
Know you at all."

Dreaming

If I catch you
When your nights are
Not as full of
Dreaming as mine,
You will not be
Able to see
Clearly as I
The dim dreamscape.

For this vision
You need night eyes
Not those day eyes
Dull from seeing.

Gemini

The fire is burning in the gas heater,
And it is too hot in the room.
He wants to light some of his new sandlewood incense,
So he takes a stick in his right hand,
Bends over the flame, and turns off the heater.

Breath

I took myself to the catch in my breath
Like a Siamese cat to her fleas.

The Trouble with my Eye, or The Reason I am Seeking Help

I was as respectful as I could be with my right eye half-closed
And a bottle of whiskey between my twisted toes,
When the Captain came in to say the Ship had run aground,
I lifted up my foot to show him what I'd found.

A Prayer: Passion

O God, I pray I might so love You
As I love the pretty girl
With the long blond hair.

The Babe Speaks my Mind

A tiny baby went in to an ecstasy of joy,
His mother held him high up by the window like a toy,
Sitting in that car there queenly plump delicious full of bliss
Tell me, now tell me, didn't she give a nice answer to my kiss?

The Ballad of Sally

Sally was the Preacher's wife,
She married him in June.
He played the great church organ,
And caught her with a tune.

Sally was a virgin wife.
She'd never known strife,
Until she found herself alone,
A good part of her life.

The Preacher was a simple man,
As earthy as the sod.
He tried to teach his people love,
And dedicate his songs to God.

But when he went to serve his flock,
He had to leave poor Sally dear,
Who sat in empty cloisters
And cried many a bitter tear.

Then one day Evangelist came
Around the church and said,
"If you don't know the love of God,
You might as well be dead."

He told her she was beautiful,
That her sadness should not be.
He spoke to her about freedom.
He said, "Sally, come with me."

The Preacher went to the church that night,
Saw Sally'd gone away,
But the Preacher still makes music, Lord!
Hear that lyrical organ play.

Writ on the Back of the Piece of Coarse Grain Sandpaper while Busy Preparing to Paint a Window, October 30, 1969

There is a little bit of modesty to say,
When I've got you pinned, stuck, six inches deep
Against the pillow, giant Y, with me inside,
I'm going to reach behind and stick my finger deep in your asshole;

And watch you cry, and kiss that cry,
And bring our giant exposition
To its grand carnival conclusion:
Giant turning thing, grand rolling coaster,
Pretty turning thing, exaltation!
Sparkling ferris-wheel, O God!
King Harvest Himself never reaped such spoil.

Greece

Do you have a minute to spare?
I have something to say that's not going to be rare,
But rather my lips kissing your lips:
O my love! My desire! All the feelings we have felt,
We must revisit, like in Greece, Cavafy's beach and tree,
Or Rihaku's landmark, as far as Cho-fu-see.

My love, your lips, I've touched, you know, before,
Our boat, you know, we've rowed before, in Greece
Where Autumn season's breezes blow exquisitely
Without questions, as in the poem you have not seen yet:
In Greece is where we'll be my love
When we make love, and lips touch, eternity.

Telepathy

Hey little girl walking by wearing red,
What do you think made me turn my head?

Divorce 2

Life has taken a turn
And I have dust on my fingers
From packing in boxes
My wife's dresses, my son's toys.

Metaphor

You are the Beach,
And I am the Tree,
But of course the Tree is the Water
That rolls on the Shore,
And asks for more
From the great Sun shining above.

The Poet Answers a Question: How He Feels about His Enemy

I'm as grateful as one can be
To one who's taught him
The meaning of Sorrow.

Song

You said you loved me and you'd never leave me
And you went with that other man.

You said you felt that we had something going
And now you're holding his hand.

You maybe love me, baby, and will never leave me, love,
But I'd sure hate to depend upon you.

My hands are dirty and my beard is growing
And the costume I'm wearing now is blue.

I'm working Sundays and painting windows Mondays
And all the time, I'm thinking of you.

I'd love to see you, babe, I'd love to hold you, love,
But I can't make no unreasonable demand.

All I can say right now is that if you were here, wow,
It would sure be grand.

To be Opened Anytime/ October 22nd

Forgetting all things Autumn,
There is something special about you.

Autumn is when all things die.

It is a new person writing this letter,
Waiting for his new bride to come home.

It wasn't just those changes that made Autumn special—
Autumn is when all things die.

There's a special breeze that blows the leaves on the trees
And off the trees along the streets and makes a sound in Autumn.

It is a new person writing this letter.

Autumn is when all things die.
It's also when my new Bride was born
And when she was married the first time four
Years ago for eternity in Autumn.
And it's the season of my birth too:

HAPPY ANNIVERSARY MY BELOVED!

O Jemila

I love you so much
Woman
Who can look like life itself
Hard and cold
As life itself
BUT
The beauty, the victory in her smile
Victory, yes!
MANSUR, the victorious
He made that smile
He loves the woman
THEY created a Prince
GAVE birth to joy.
JEMILA—you are wife to two men.

Three Lines Where There Are the Wrong Number of Syllables per Line to be Haiku, and It Is also One Syllable Short of Haiku

The wind is blowing the trees.
Lo, a branch is broken.
God is love.

Lust

Cassandra sank one thousand ships,
Lest one hardy fellow go by.

Poems from MUTU KUBLA ANTA MUTU, Die before Death (1974)

Madzubiat

The Madzub has always been in love with the angel.
He sees the angel in the eyes of beautiful women.
The light and love of beautiful women.

The Bow and Arrow

A progression of images during this concentration,
The objects themselves: a bow, an arrow, lying there.

A bow with arrow stretching, side view,
Then back view,
Shooting and hitting the bull's eye.

Then you are the target.
Arrows in the heart.
Bow and arrow broken.

Consideration of the shooter and the target,
Their qualities, the fitness of the shooter,
The worthiness of the target.
Finally, a warrior, holding bow and arrows in right hand,
Counting beads with the left.

The Retreat

O what a wonderful retreat!
Up on the Hillside!
With all the comforts of home
And gentle breezes blowing through the windows.

The sun itself making bright and shining appearances,
Backed up by an ensemble of blue, blue skies.
Oh! What a retreat!
That those ascetics up on Chamonix
Could revel in such domestic solitude
Looked after by a loving wife.

Sita followed Rama for twelve years in the woods during his
Vanavasa, which means roaming in the woods.
Nakhra has Mansur for ten days, inshallah [God-willing]
as she's never had him before.

What more?
Inshallah, inshallah, inshallah
Bismillah! [in the name of Allah] Complètementé. [It's done!]
FIKR OF THE DHIKR 100 TIMES WITH CONCENTRATION ON
THE
THE BOW AND THE ARROW.

The Runway (1)

This afternoon, "Jesus Christ Superstar" and "Hey Joe, here comes your friend," greeted me down at one end of the block.

On the back stretch a black girl wearing dark glasses took me gently by the arm and started walking along with me.

She asked, "You alright? You alright?"

She touched my heart. I mustered a smile and looked at her. Yes, the look was a darshan.

"You'll be alright now," she said, as she retreated and continued her path the opposite way I was going.

The kids at the corner store said, "Hare Krishna, Hare Krishna," as I walked by.

Musings 1

I write to keep from forgetting; meaning, if I write it, I won't have to remember to write when I remember I wanted to write something but can't remember what it was.

+

Mansur, why do you perform your practices now with your right arm always up?
So that I do not forget the time I could not raise up my arm.

Doesn't it get trying, always counting beads with that arm slightly raised or holding tashbih with left hand or just in that mudra you make with your fists?
Yes, but I do not want to forget the time when I could not raise up my arm.

+

My prayer cap is from Murshid.
My beads are from Vilayat.
About the rest, my lips are sealed.

+

Before I met Pir Vilayat he used to say
Mansur this, Mansur that. Then, one
day, he didn't say 'Mansur' any more.
He said , "Al-Hallaj this, Al-Hallaj that."

+

How to see without seeing?

Be so absorbed in your own vision
Of beauty that you cannot,
You simply will not,
Give it up for something less beautiful.

133

+

"Take this cup from me Lord."
I didn't bring you a cup. You brought a bowl.
Mansur bows down.
What's the matter?
"I'm afraid."
Don't be afraid.

The Runway (7)

My robe is from Kuwait.
My incense is from India.
My rain suit is from Korea.
My Murshid was from San Francisco.
My Pir is on a mountain in France.
About the rest, my lips are sealed.

A Yawn!

O Yes!
I call it a visit from the devil.
Satan whispered in my ear, *you can quit early. You are in good shape.*
I answer:
Until the blood shot is out of my eyes,
Until the white is gone from my throat,
Until the right lung has no cordillera,
Until the kidneys do not ache from sitting in posture,
Until the solar plexus is a sea of fire,
Until the heart is radiating light,
Until the song of Rumi describes me,
I will not flee.

Ya Alim

It [Ya Alim] ferrets out dark corners.
It brings light where there is darkness.
It chips away at the cavern walls.
It scrapes stalactites from the cavern ceiling.
It drills holes where the dynamite goes.
It blows the wall apart.
It scrapes cookie dough dried in a bowl.
It chips peanut butter stuck in arrears.
It chisels cobwebs crystalline dark.
It scraps waffles thrown in the park.
It goes *zip zoom buzz buzz.*
It goes *oush oush rub a dub dub.*
It goes *eeeyow eeeeyow.*
Yow yow eeeeeeee pow.
It makes the red in the eyes go away.
It makes the red from the flies go play.
The red in the eyes are the *yow* in the *pow.*
E makes the *pow* makes the *yow growl.*
We mean business you flunky letters.
Get up there and do your job.

The Mystic's Goal

Fana-fi-Allah is the immediate goal.
Annihilation in Allah.
Baqi-bi-Allah is the desired state.
Everyday life in Allah.
All for the benefit of humanity.
All for the love of my wife.
All for the upliftment of humanity.
I want to be fit. I want to serve.
I am listening God.
The voices, the influences, all those who would hold me back "for love,"
They all are what they are.
It does not matter ...
You are leading me.
You are showing me the Path through all of that.
You are doing it.
You are telling it.
I am trying to receive it like your puppet.
You pull the strings.
You say the words.
You, You, You.
I'm looking for You.
I'm coming for You.
I want to be one with You.
I WANT TO KNOW MYSELF.
(Because I've been told you are none other than my self.)

Musings 2

GOD SAID

"What about the adept's posture?"

Mansur said, "I am happy sitting like a king."

+

GOD SAID

Eat, last night so I ate.
I was too weak to meditate
Too awake to sleep.

God is the Sea: The Way They All Came In

This poem, which came in a dream, I considered as God's answer to my
deep longing to know Her. Mansur

The way everything came in—
Like the waves, with the waves, in waves—
Makes me cry.

And when we put the sunset together,
They all had their place.
Even pulling them out of the river
And burying them in the family plot,
They all had their place.
They were so happy to go,
Even though they were just
A piece of glass and a tire full of mud.
They were my great Aunt Clara and my Grandfather Klemm.

The way everything came in,
When it was time for dinner,
Like the waves, with the waves, in waves
Makes me cry.

The way they all came in,
They were all so sad.
They were all so hungry,
Like some people for dinner.
They all knew Her—
Old family friends.
Here comes a clump of grass.

They way they all come in,
Like the waves, in waves.
They all come, and they're nice,
Like the cows wound up for pasture.
They all come in at sundown,
Like the waves, with the waves.

They are all so obedient.

They don't smile. They don't frown.
But they're all so sad,
When they come in, in waves.

And when we put the sunset together,
I have to bless it with my foot,
To get the joy back in the colors,
To get the life back in the death.

And when we put the sunset together,
Laying side by side on the sand,
And the lifeless get some color,
And the rocks begin to shine,
O! I can't help from crying.
No, I can't help from crying,
As the colors take their shapes,
And the outlines start to glow,
And the picture starts to show.
O! What would it do without us?
Ah! What joy would show in all creation,
If our breath weren't there to blow,
To breathe, and bless, and paint for life
The joy, the cow, coming in like creation,
In waves, with the waves, like the waves?

The way everything comes in—
As I was sitting with my Beloved,
I was just a little jealous.
They were all returning to be with Her.
There was no way to stop them.
They were all part of Her total picture,
Part and parcel now returning.
They were all so obedient;
Yet they couldn't get off the movement;
Yet they really had no choice.
They just came in, with the waves.
They just came in, on the waves.
They were tired, and they weren't smiling;
Yet they came on just the same.
It was that it was the sundown,
And the breath of light was gone.

Epilogue after Attar

O Mansur! You have scattered on the world the contents of the vessel of the musk of secrets. The horizons of the world are full of your perfumes and lovers are disturbed because of you. Your verses are your seal, and they are known as *Mutu Kubla Anta Mutu* or Die Before Death. These conferences and talks and discourses are the stages of the way of bewilderment; or, one may say, they are the works of intoxication. Enter into this work with love.

When the Duldul of your love gallops and you desire something, act in conformity with your desire. Love is the remedy for all ills, and it is the remedy of the soul in the two worlds. O you, who have set out on the path of inner development, do not read my book only as an adventure or as a novel, but read it with some understanding; and for this a man must be hungry for something, dissatisfied with himself and this world.

He who has not smelled the perfume of my discourse has not found the way of lovers. But he who will read it with care will become active and will be worthy to enter the way of which I speak. Those of the outer world will be like drowned men as regards my discourse; but those of the inner world will understand its secrets. My book is the ornament of its time. It is at once a gift for distinguished men and a boon for the common. If a man as cold as ice reads this book, he will shoot forth as fire out of the veil which hides the mystery from him. My writings have an astonishing peculiarity— they give more profit according to the manner in which they are read. If you ponder over them often, they will benefit you more each time. The veil of this wife of the harem will be drawn aside for you only gradually in the place of honor and grace.

I have scattered pearls from the ocean of contemplation. I am thereby acquitted, and this, my book, is the proof. But if I praise myself too much, you may not approve, though he who is impartial will recognize (*inshallah*) my merit, for the light of my full moon shall not be hidden God-willing. If I am not remembered for myself, I shall be remembered until the resurrection by the pearls of poetry that God has scattered on the heads of men.

Reader, if you experience some wellbeing through having read this poem with attention, remember God in your prayers.

He has strewn here and there roses from the garden. Remember him well,

O my friends! Each teacher reveals his ideas in his own special way, and then he disappears. Like my predecessors, God has revealed the bird of my soul to those who are asleep. Perhaps the sleep which fills your life has deprived you of this discourse, but having met it, your soul will be awakened by the secret which it reveals.

And now my brain is smoked like a niche where stands a light. I have said to myself, "O you, who talk so much, instead of so much talking, say your beads and search the secrets. What is the use of all these narrations to men corrupted with egotism? What can come out of hearts taken up with vanity and self-pride?"

If you wish the ocean of your soul to remain in a state of salutary movement, you must die to all your old life, and then keep silence. (The Conference of the Birds)

JOURNAL POEMS (1976)

All Things Die Stalking a Rabbit on Foot

A list for the following day in his head,
The self-made man went to bed.
Things he was going to do on his spread
And things he was thinking and things he had read.
Unlike the factory man who just makes lead,
He just puts his head in bed,
And stalks a rabbit on foot.

Water

When you think about water,
If you're a Buddhist,
You know all things die.
You sit by a river at night
And you see in the reflection
Of the lights on the water
That the river is moving.

What is a glassful? Or
A particle of water in a grain of sand?

Wet sand. Dry sand.
Where did the water go?
In the sky.

Is it still water in the sky?
Was it still water when it was wet sand?
No. It was not water.

But is not the water vapor in the sky still water?
And some say it forms clouds,
And when it gets heavy,
It rains down on the whole town and country too.

Is it raining everywhere in the world when it is raining here?
It was pretty hard to conceive of once.
Something like wondering why there isn't a bridge across the ocean.
How could anything man-made be that large?

Technology

The stereophonic nature of earphones is ultimate sound.
Amplified ears.
A 135 mm lens amplification with a big A.

Get your bowling shirts today
With extra large pockets for your phones.
You'll tune out once,
More than twice you'll have a ball.
Take your position
And bowl.

A Baby

How we are part of all things is come by thinking about the cycle of life, for example, by looking at a sleeping baby. Soon he will not sleep. He will be alive, among the living, talking, acting like a person. Then he will be like a child again, an old wrinkled man pissing in his bed.

Sleeping now he is birth term plus 11 days. Think back to his germination period. From proto-matter liquid he grew. As he decays after death, he will become matter somewhere in the vastness of the universe.

The baby 11 days old pushes and pushes with his feet until his head rests against the side of his crib. The firmness with his head against it gives him security. He is all head; his head is all his world. With itself at rest against something firm, it rests.

American babies are kind of on a throne. The society is baby centered rather than self-centered. Because of the lack of sense of self, people are prepared to give. They feel moral because giving is a moral Christian religious virtue. They tithe; they have charities. Yet sometimes unrealistic parent-serving schedules are imposed upon babies who ultimately rule.

A baby carried with the parent, pressed against something firm, fed immediately upon request, is not sacrificed to the living necessities of the parents, themselves people who know who they are.

A Dual Pronouncement from the American Association of Broadcasters

Kids are impressionable. They may see bad guys, but they won't see them in the roles of heroes. They will learn that crime doesn't pay.

Little did we know the proponents of marijuana presented their case last night. We shall make efforts to oppose, nay, strangle this propaganda so opposed to the American way.

The News

If you catch me writing, "The news is black comedy," know I watch it
for material. Some actors used to watch life, I watch TV. I'm a tele-vac.
I vacuum the television. Tell me the news is something else, like The
Carter Family, and that you're a folk music archivist. You know, today on
the news they had a stock market archivist on the program. He'd read all
those Dow-Jones averages, which consists of 30 selected industrials, rails,
hogs, and mines, and he thinks that the Dow-Jones Industrial averages
are an adequate barometer of prices. But some new guys want to take the
average of the entire industry, since over 12,000 stocks are registered on the
exchange. And how could just 30 be an adequate barometer? I don't know.

Musings 3

I would like to take a picture of the song coming out of the Victrola.

+

August is such a funny way of life. I have these funny ways of marking ends and marking time, of cycles and completions. I don't want to take the time of finishing. It comes to me now in June that August shortly passes.

+

You feel it here (filling his chest), then your lungs begin to feel like balloons, and you start to float off, until somebody says "Hey, you little red balloon."

+

To say philosopher Jean-Paul Sartre went to the country home of an obscure mouth harp player who didn't say hello is as plausible as Bob Dylan sitting on Etta Baker's front porch while she played "Three Blind Mice" flawlessly.

+

There's a new kind of blacksmith in town. No one knows for sure how long he's been around. He's the man who takes pictures, and now makes portraits, "does commercial work," and sells photo supplies. He's a bystander, brother.

+

A bird in the hand is worth two in the bush.

"It means half is better than not any," said Denny.

"I think it means something in your hand rather than something in the bush," said Niki.

If somebody asked me, I'd say, "Why would I want a bird in my hand?"

My Last Letter

Concatenation of accumulation,
The family man, book of poems
On subjects lived
Zen-like everyday,
While pursuing,
Not enduring,
Joy and ecstasy.

These are Wednesday's jobs,
And the epistolary dispute with the university.

They come or go like Wednesday's jobs:
To dig or borrow a car to
Drive to the base of the mountain.
I will have borrowed snow shoes
To climb to shoot the film
Concerned with
A journey to
The top of Mount
Marquette and inter-
Spliced (shot actually)
With self portraits
Of myself,
Walking out on a long breakwater,
Being smashed by giant waves
Breaking there in a storm.

This is my second warning, my last letter.

Nocturnal Landscape

The great Mexican pleasure bath,
You just come in and lie down,
In front of a low rise
Set of bleachers where the others
Wait their turn,
Under the open-ended tent,
Open as it happens
As an advertisement,
For the others walking by
As I was
With what must have been all my faculties.
But everyone was too friendly
To pass by ... I couldn't anyway,
And so I lay
And felt my body bathed
With touching tender finger mouths
And nodded my approval,
Somewhat embarrassedly,
And gave up, somewhat reluctantly,
Almost childishly really,
A spasm that licked her ear
And spotted my bed
Dream.

I Forget

Traveling
With everything under the sun
In my arms, I was looking for someone,
A friend's girl friend,
Probably just an excuse to be hanging around
In labyrinths of magazine stands
And train schedules,
Stopping
For just a moment
To watch the basketball game,
As I was around the auditorium,
Behind the bleachers
In the balcony
At the rail on the main floor
A special seat right in front of the basket ...
My, what action!
But it couldn't be—
It must be—
A film in front of my eyes.
But what was her name again?

Dedicated to Lee Harvey Oswald, "I'm just a patsy," he said to take the Fall for the CIA's Coup D'Etat of the U.S. Government in 1963. RIP JFK.

I must prophesy:
"We are doomed,"
The result of inexorable logic
If everything is the way it is.

It is our responsibility
The wars exist.

We talk about honorable peace.
Words.

We fight.
The president asks for money.
Money.

The Congress gives it.
The Defense Department spends it.
Bombs.

We elect our Congress, as the Constitution insists.
I rarely vote for the winners,
Who represent the will of the people.

Sexual Reality

Let me tell you about sexual reality.
Can't you leave sex out of this?
Its unreality stems from experience
The ...

Excuse me, I see that there is a train coming.
I'll call back over at the station,
After the engine with its
Circus insignia passes, pulling
Boxcars marked
A SEXUAL ATTRACTION
THE MYSTERY
And then the caboose.

Hart Crane, Where were you at?

Your words are so strange; namely,

"VIII. Atlantis

Music is then the knowledge of that which relates to love in harmony and system.
Plato

Through the bound cable strands, the arching path
Upward, veering with light, the flight of strings—
Taut miles of shuttling moonlight syncopate
The whispered rush, telepathy of wires."

Walt Whitman
I think I know where you were at.

Herman Melville
I know where you were at.

No I don't,
Neither of you,

Nor Hart Crane either.

Eternity

One word after
Another,
Step by step,
We travel toward
Eternity.

Halt this privacy,
Prophesy,
Philosophizing,

As the eyeball, retina, brain, mind
Focuses on the sanctuary of the heart,
Above the landing,
Up a short stairway,
At each of the four points
Between all four corners

Beyond heartbeats.

Path to Spirit

Starting out is not difficult.
Afterwards,
Airplanes fly
Lost pilots
Land
Ho.

A Life's Path

Hungry, but too impatient to eat,
I entered a Zen Buddhist monastery
For seven years.

Separated by the handle of a shovel
I hoed the necessary garden
For a while.

Separated by the handle of a shovel
From the earth I am
Today.

March 24, 1967

Honesty resolution:
Catharsis.

Epiphany:
The end of feeling.

An intellectual responsibility
To read E.H.
Gombrich's *Art and Illusion*.

Social pressure is related to honesty,
In that it moves the center off
Center to nowhere,
But out there
Somewhere like

The silent horn in the high school band.

People like that
Make people like us
Go on worth living.

Musings 4

Will you look down on me
Because I am dispossessed?

If you listen,
That is where you will see me,

My claw marks
Screeching.

+

Music is
Somebody playing the harp
Of your mind delicately.

"Oh, he's alright;
The room's just a different color for him."

+

I was going down the street
And my two feet did beat
A salute on the policeman's headache.

+

A guy came over to our house.
He lost his head,
But we found it for him.
We gave it promptly back,
And he went home with it.
And then he asked for his pants.
We didn't have them, but we gave him some.
It's a good thing too.
It was snowing out.

3rd Eye

I, I, I,
I am a me-first
Selfish
Unthoughtful,
Unmindful of others ...

You! Walt Whitman,
Under my feet,
In the color of the sky between the branches,

What universe escaped your yin yang bulldozer?

A Definition of Great

I don't care.
You choose them.
All great men were turned on.

What does "great" mean?

Great is being turned on,
And being
Modest enough, to go on
Being
Turned on.

I Don't Know What to Call this One?

Haight Street in San Francisco is love.
And love is news.

Who said LSD is news?
I don't know,
And you feel an obligation
To ask why?
Because you think he wants to say
Tim Leary, that's why.

So tonight I said to my wife
Who was that sheriff in Central City?
And she says Central City? What's that?
And I say, surprised she doesn't know, Colorado,
The place with the face on the ballroom floor.

And I'm thinking of
Annie Oakley and know
Howard Keel and Betty
Grable or Betty Hutton
Played the part in
Carousal.

That girl sheriff
Came after Wild Bill
Hickok who was shot when
He turned his back to
The door. He,
Wild Bill,
Had long hair.

It's a kind of working back in history to the roots of America,
When villainy was in flower,
And violence was born,
As a defense mechanism
Against the vengeful, wrathful nature.

Talking about another

Eon's bag, in another's
Language, won't hurt
Scholarly appreciation.

The Ashtray Episode

A small child leaves
A tiny brass ashtray in the hall
And goes for a crawl
In the same room I am.

I take the ashtray out of sight
Which is my way out of proportion right.

My child returns and,
Missing his ashtray,
Meets face to face for the first time
The mysterious.

Listen, Listen

Listen, echoes the voice in the picture
Of the blue sky.

God, says the little child, lives up there
In the blue sky.

The picture changes. The man watches.
The rain falls.

Seasons change, as predicted,
All remains.

A Word Thing

"Very strange,"
McLuhan says, "Young people today
Want roles, not goals."

And me?
I get insecure when I don't have my role.
I'm insecure now.
I'm leaving teaching.
I guess I'm going out looking for a goal?

Insights are weird, strange, verbal constructs.
I realize I need an exterior structure,
For security;
For example, I'm in school, I have a job, I'm a teacher—
Roles
Yikes
Stock responses
Yikes
Words
Yikes
Language
Yikes

Rules make the role intelligible, make life static, make habits and laws
safeguards for   insecure people.

Tonight I told my wife what *Notes from Underground* was about:
Words: the inadequacy of language.
No one agrees.
Once again I feel different,
At odds with "the system."
Then I realize:
That's what genius is. Anarchist. Activist.
First, he realizes that he is at odds with the system,
Self-consciousness.
And then he feels anxious about it,
Anxious.
Then he realizes that he is a system,

Knowledge.
And he reveals it to the world,
Creates it some say,
But it's more like uncovering it.
Creates or uncovers ... words
Yikes.

Dear Rock 'N Rollers

What a gassy thing *not* to wonder anymore:
What am I *going* to do?
What do I *want* to do?
When it's your self,
And it's what *can* I do,
And what size audience am I?

The bag of everything in the world is a poem;
However, there is a real loss of the aesthetic sense,
Hung up on knowledge, theorizing,
Not poem making.

In spite of that, my head riveted
On a beam of vibrations,
Strung between my ears,
Peers.

Smooth Pebbles

Son of my flesh
Has sensed my impatience
With his progress.
Lately we confront one another
Animal to animal.
He is moving,
Learning
To crawl.

Early Lesson in the Primer toward Attaining

Breathing is important in poem reading.
Strange as it seems,
The in-taking and the out-taking of breath
Causes a considerable change in the harmonies
Of the intonation level,
Leaving the reader somewhat uneasy.

Jasmine Blind

And when the music stopped
Snow white,
What then?

Out past the ruins of an ash,
White ruin,
Again?

Out poking into crowds
Of leaves
And men.

And the light that she
Left on
For me.

Her signal lights and signs
My way.
I stumble, crawl and scratch my way—

But I must have lost her in all these lights.
It's a nice city, sure, that keeps its lights on
All night long, for a guy lost out on the town.

A Conversation

Bird cages, 100 of them,
In his hand right up in front ...
In the air,
All welded and patched and pasted together,
Delicate equilibrium balanced by their own weight,
Teetering, e-a-s-y
Does it, yellow
Peckers at the patches pecking
Tick, tick.
And me here across the room,
Peck, peck, a yellow pecker
Building a boulder from a bubble
Pip
Pip
At the place
Where the pebble falls
In vision uncaged.

Poem Round, Don't Lose Track

Sung to the tune of "Three Blind Mice."
See how they run.
They all run after the farmer's wife,
Who cut off their tails with a carving knife.
Poor blind mice,
Poor blind mice,
See how they run,
See how they run,
They all run after the farmer's wife,
They all run after the farmer's wife,
Who cut off their tails with a carving knife,
Who cut off their tails with a carving knife,
Poor blind mice,
Poor blind mice,
Poor blind mice.

Only when it's done, it sounds like

Don't lose track
Don't lose track
Don't lose track don't lose track don't lose track
Don't lose track don't lose track don't lose track
Don't lose track
Don't lose track
Don't lose track
Don't lose track
Don't lose track don't lose track don't lose track
Don't lose track don't lose track don't lose track
Don't lose track don't lose track don't lose track
Don't lose track don't lose track don't lose track
Don't lose track
Don't lose track
Don't lose track
Don't lose track
Don't lose track
Don't lose track
Don't lose track don't lose track don't lose track
Don't lose track don't lose track don't lose track

Don't lose track don't lose track don't lose track

For a long, long time.

The Game of Life

In the rocking chair room
The ladies sewing circle
Got together
To discuss a tennis game.

They all had their score books.
And one lady said, My fault,
And they all took note.
One said, Let's keep score the rest of our lives.

There was no objection, and all assumed
They'd all keep score and count up their tally
At a later date,
Until one remarked that they wouldn't really know

Until the autopsy. They all agreed
Cancer ought to have his say:
The first one who dies
Wins.

Organization

The streets are bumpy;
They are narrow & bumpy,
And the traffic lights are not synchronized.

There are incentives for things like that.
If you work, you can be an All-American city.
If you paved the streets and synchronized the lights,

But when you go around, and the streets are bumpy
& narrow, and the traffic lights are not synchronized; and,
The towns are crummy. You know nobody needs to do anything.

Poetry is Ageless

"And the reader was a listener," went one of his lines.
Whose lines?
"Why the old man's lines,
The grand old man's lines left upon a washboard
One day in early May in the year of our Lord
One thousand nine hundred and sixty six."
This dates the poem; and the poet who is 25.

Just yesterday really.

Loss or Flight

Who understands the burning house?
I do not care about the factory,
Nor do I care about the drive-in movie.
The root beer stand is expendable.

Think, however, about leaving Vancouver
For Montreal on a train
Because your house burned down

And, seeing up ahead of you,
The sky in flames,

Even with your eyes shut.

Conversation

It all started with a negative.
I think I'm going to leave you.
But in the same breath,
I think I'm right where I want to be.
I like the domestic situation.
I don't like to be alone.
I couldn't be better than I am right now.

Why did I want to leave you?
I don't know.

To look for somebody better,
Somebody to love me more?

You need more than one?

Guru

Holy people can know when they're
Going to die by the way their motor boat heart thumps.

When it's slowing down,
Soon the distance
Between up and down
Is so wide, it coincides
With breath,
And everything
Thumps just once.

Meditation

O! The bloodless hand,
Hanging from my knee,
Is mine.

Another Paranoid Vision

Some bulls busted into my house the other night.
I was sitting naked
With my camera by my side.
I snatched off the lens cover
And jacked the lens up and let
Fly with a shot.

And they grabbed me,
And they beat me,
And they threatened to kill me,
And they kicked me,
And they cursed me,
And they threatened to castrate me,
And they threw me in jail,

And they said, "We'll show those mobs they can't rule our town.
We got his film."

All sung to the tune of *My Dog has Fleas*.

Musings 5

A man I know makes himself
Indispensable to his wife
And tries to make his Company love him.

He fails
To make his Company love him,
And his wife lives with him,
And they make love,
Telling the Company to fuck itself.

+

A baby has lots of bubbles in his body.
That's why you have to come around fairly often to burp the babe.
But just as much as it seems you're coming around a lot
The little nipper little by little learns
To fend for himself,
And you find yourself with just a little more time
To yourself.

+

The mercury beam street light
Catches and holds your eye
Like a medallion in the sky.

+

Life is a woman.
I cannot help the allegory.
I feel her.

+

I want to write about the sort of death
I take each day. When did you first take it?
And why? I hear it in the deep heart's core,
A million watery miles from shore,

A drawing in the drawing of my cigarette,
A hand clutching one word more.

The Queen

The queen talks about her little houseboy in
An intimate passage that the queen asked to be left out
Of the recent book about her late husband that was
Referred to in newspaper publicity as a "love letter."

"You'll just be my little houseboy,
Following me around wherever I go,
Carrying in the groceries,
Opening car doors,
Doing the dishes,
Cleaning the house,
Taking care of the baby,
Doing the laundry and taking it to the dryer.
All those things and fucking me."

Legal Suit about a Baked Potato

There once was a man, who said,
"It's old, too steamy, not worth eating, send it back,"
And a waiter who said,
"You must pay, Sir."
"I will not," the man said,
And was sued by them.

Day of court came, and he said,
"I say it's a bad potato."
"Conceded," they said. "But, Sir,
They say steaming is the only way to keep it warm."
And they won.

And the moral is:
Know what time the potatoes are cooked,
And don't be much later to the restaurant.
And watch out for the dilemma of the man
Who left his trial saying,
"We got there when the restaurant opened."

Panegyric to Kirk's Panacea

Kirk, visitor
From around the world,
Slap my forehead
Like a Pole,
If you aren't the strongest sound,
Then Krishna can't come around
No more. I smoke my joint
And don't worry at all
About the fire insurance,
Which takes too much endurance.

But I'm digressing Kirk, visitor
From around the world.
It's a Ho! Ho! Ho! and
Here we go.
From New York
Round to San Francisco,
The long way,
On your own
Without a phone,
Amazing how
The meaning of
Your own
Is one word

Alone.

Gossip

A guy I know has the greatest love scene going.
Everything's coming his way with no give and take between the middle
man.
It's a pure romantic fairy tale
In reality come true,
And the only cancellation
Is for me because of you.

Be Safe on the Road, My Love

Driving your old used car
And keeping to the tight mountain road

VISITING FRIENDS

How would it sound forever,
If every time I took my leave,
And as I was making my way home
Through total autumn,
You knew you would call after me,
Take it easy and don't get busted, man?

Prejudice

The problem with all the Max Raffertys in the world,
They're all over the place,
In the majority everywhere,
In the conspiracy against Jesus,
Marching lockstep,
Stilt-legged with Hitler's thugs.
The war was a big success.
WE WON.
It was a gala affair, and a good time was had by all.
Like fun you did.
You did it.
From now on, there shall be no reward for kindness.
All those in favor,
Die.

The Great Game

In the West, here, there are rational ways of understanding things
like art. In spite of people repeating *words can't express this.*

It's all part of the Great Game.
Remember Rudyard Kipling's Kim.
After all, he acquired merit by giving intuition to me,
The Tibetan monk in his life.

The Great Game's rules:
Stay inside the law.
Dress for the occasion.

The ties that bind. The great money navel cord. Money, money.
After money, before money. How you get it. What you do. You.

After satisfaction, after groceries are bought, after life insurance is
paid for, after car insurance is paid for, after federal income tax is
paid for, after personal property insurance is paid for, after the rent.
What?

That place is where you are.
After hobbies, after noon,
After hell at the cell, the cosmic energy dance.
That is where you are.

Your true self left behind.

A Woman Replies to a Man

Stoned freak,
Spastic indeterminate whiz bang,
I can only speak for myself ... today,
Work, work, work a cigarette,
Work, work, work, yourself to death.
Having all kinds of fun, wish you were here.
I breathe in. I breathe out.
Let's not let my descriptions stand in the way of a whole friendship.

Niki

Like I told you before, words can't express it, only this time how I feel
about you, all of the space you take up, and tonight how I need to
touch you, and feel you respond.

O awkward angel, let your hair down, come closer, crowd my head.
Slowly pressure, push, unlike all the unhappy, blind, no wheres.

Bring along your guitar, and your fine pointed pen, and draw with
your eyes shut, draw parallel lines, that meet, right here in space,
your space, where I am, crowded and vacant for you.

You know how warm the light is in the window of the house on the
hill where you live?

You know what the massive hollow reverberating sound of the heavy
steel door opening is?

You know the pressure of your father's undelivered caress beneath
desire?

You know the landscape loneliness of the Greek land, sea, sky,
conspiracy?

You know love disappointed, and condoned, and revived, barely
shaken to its roots?

O dear one, what can I do for you tonight?
Is there stuff between your legs needs loving?
Musty, bloody, brain cream, foldy hair flesh,
Is there stuff between your legs needs titillating?

Yea, satori in the flesh has yet to come.
You might say the second coming is expected,
Not so much hoped for as desired,
Not so much needed as wanted,

Like when the great dream is dwarfed by the real thing.
That's when your hard aches begin.

That's when it starts all over again.
That's out of my field.

I am now, for sure.

The Spider

I first saw it this morning,
Sitting in the tub,

A spider crawling in my bathtub,
The only shoe on my foot.

Who wants to squash a spider in their tub?
I turned on the water.

He wouldn't be washed down; he
Wouldn't slip; he wouldn't drown.

He wouldn't die.
I went away. My wife will handle him.

Sitting next to the tub this afternoon
I saw the spider crawling.

My wife said, "He was there this morning."
He must not die, I said,

And picked him up with the afternoon mail,
And we went outside.

And I look at him closely.
I didn't count his legs.

He fell off my mail. He didn't fall actually.
He hung, lower and lower,

Until I walked off the porch,
Inside the house with my mail,

Tangled with his residue
I couldn't leave anywhere else.

A Fantasy

I had a fantasy
That lasted & lasted & lasted
And came out the other end
At the same place.

I answered the telephone,
And a man wanted to give me a job.
I said, "I had another offer last Saturday,
For more money at a prettier place."

He said, "I'll give you more
And make your rank higher. I can't
Do anything about the place."

So I called the other man
And he said, "I'll give you more
And up your rank and, well,
You know the place."

I had a fantasy.

Excess

Do you think you'll be able to sleep?
No.
Then why don't you have a sandwich. It'll
Make you tired enough to sleep.
I'm tired enough to sleep, I just can't sleep.

Aw, you know what I've always said,
"If you can't sleep, you aren't
Tired enough."

Really I can't.

Imagine Groucho Marx
Going to The National Association of Psychiatrists' meeting,
And, after a big introduction about how here was Dr. Marx to read a
paper
Containing a new insight into dipsomania,
Him saying, "I always tell my patients, if they
Can't sleep, they aren't tired enough."

Birth

It's no use telling why I wept,
When I saw my son.

It's because I had no father.
I envied him.

Blue Flower

The Zen book of ethics fell into my hands the other day.
I read it, and here's what it had to say:

It said watch those illusions,
Keep to the pathway,
Guard against identity,
Toss a tulip at insanity.

My World

My world—

Is essence chisel-faced and
Sad-eyed
Fantasy/acorn.

My world—

A glazed eyeball
Cranking & cranking & cranking
An old model.

My world—

There is much chaos.
You must let it pass.
There is nothing to fear.

The Misfit

I went into a clothing store the other day.
There was a suede jacket on the rack,
Just like I'd been wanting
For a long time.
And it even had a fur lining.

I thought that was strange, because it gets hot indoors
Even with a jacket on sometimes.
And they told me it was an outside jacket.
And they told me that it fit me like an indoor jacket.

Love Song

Baby, what you do to me is something like
What electricity did to the United States,
And what Telestar did for television,
Blew me up big as a balloon,
Only to prick me with the good ole amen blues
Aaaammmmen.

Music Program

I feel like Jessie Fuller.
You don't know him?
Have you ever heard the San Francisco Bay Blues?

Then here's Jack Elliott playing it.
Doesn't Jack Elliott sound a lot like
Early Bob Dylan?

Here he is doing *I Want You.*
Isn't that a lot more relaxing than this chipmunk sound,
Like a 45 record playing on 78?

Here's something else by a man who died recently
Of an overdose of heroin.

It acts on your mind like
It's a love song, but it's just the opposite.

You go mad,
Or get famous in your mind.

Hemorrhoids Cure

It might have something to do
With the amount of time I spend on the toilet.
It isn't natural I believe.

But now that they're here,
I wonder just why they came?
Those bulging veins.

Is it because I sit so much?
Have I been letting off too much steam?
Is it absolutely necessary for me to have them?

Is it because you haven't kissed me
For sometime that I know I can carry them,
And they won't hurt?

Two Marriages

There's a reason I'm with her,
And not with her.

Just the same, there's a reason
For her being with him.

I just don't know what it is yet.

Fairy Tale

Once I had a hobby.
It was a very expensive one.
I left it for awhile.

When I came back, my step-father
Had sold my expensive equipment.
I never went back again.

Now I want to go back again.
I can go back now,
Because I have accepted him loving my mother.

What his love for her
Is, is not what mine was.

Now it still is,
But I will buy my own equipment.

It is expensive.
You don't ride a hobby.

You horse it until it is
Just exactly what it is.

Question

Two ground squirrels
Play together and look alike
But sleep in different beds.

Can people lie together
Who play together
Without committing adultery?

Or to put it another way,
Am I happily married?

Not Yet

Sticks and stones
Will break my bones,
But words,
They cannot hurt me.

I am strong as snowflake.
I am hard and round as bone itself.
I am all those places
You felt out of me.

Que tal? How are you?

I am fine, thank you.
I am where the furniture was
When you saw it move,
Trying to sneak up on a one track mind.

I have a message.
It is sticks and stones.

Otis's Song

What do people think of you?
I don't know. Strange, I guess.
He doesn't give a shit, says Lou.
Beautiful, says Judy.
A fine madness, says Carl.
A jerk, says Niki.
A good man for the profession, says Murray.
Under lots of pressure moving his family, having a baby
Making important career decisions, says Peter.
He's an acid head, says Kirk.
Funny guy, says Jack.
Screwed up, says Mary.
Great, says Marty.
Just Otis, says Ruth.
I don't know, says Otis, let's see now.
What's happening? Upsy daisy, look out, watch
Out, around the barn, oh where, oh where,
Free for all, 2 by 4, screened in porch,
Watch out, let's see, what do people think of *you*?

12 WILD HORSES ON THE ROAD TO NEW MEXICO (1996)

12 Wild Horses on the Road to New Mexico

The highway between Three Points and Mule Creek
Joins Arizona and New Mexico.

I took it on the way to Santa Fe,
And I am taking it on the way back to Tucson.

Now I understand why the saint from North Africa—
His name is Alawi—
Always took the same road into the town
And back home again.

12 wild horses meeting me—
Just like all day I am meeting my thoughts
Deposited on the road along the way
On the trip over.

Al-Alawi
All the time thinking of God
Meets his joy on the way back home.

While me,
An agony of anger and upset,
Keeps me reacting
Stomach tight
Emotion rising, like a stomach ache.

I have passed the Very Large Array
On the Plains of Agustin.
28 giant radio-telescopes,
Weighing 230 tons each,
Blocking the ancient longhorn driveway
Stretching all the way
In a Y-shape
From Horse Springs and Datil 125 miles,
All the way to Magdalena,
Which peaked in 1919,
When 150,000 sheep
And 21,677 cattle

Walked to the railroad at Magdalena.

The thoughts of upset grew boils on my back
And neck by the time I reached Santa Fe.
And while 28 radio-telescopes received messages
From outer space that there is water
200 million light years away in Markarian 1,
I receive my own fire.

And when I approach the border mountains,
I am aghast.
The strange fire rising vertically
Is not Phelps-Dodge in Tyrone smelting copper,
Even though I labeled the smell in the air
30 miles away "smelter."
It is not the Morenci mine,
North of Three Points doing Wednesday's work.
It is the mountain burning pink smoke.

My own fire burns before my eyes,
As I slow my truck
To allow 12 wild horses to pass—
Some with shoes, some without—
In my lane,
Trotting to New Mexico.
They pass,
And I resume my drive,
Expecting to see cowboys chasing the horses,
Envious of Alawi,
As I receive all the way to Tucson
The burning thoughts I'd seeded
On the way to Santa Fe.

There are no chasing cowboys,
Only these angry flowers
Collected by the sower of the seeds alone,
This unhappy gardener.

After the letter of forgiveness was written by the side of the road,
I answer myself finally, "I wrote that letter already.

It is complete now. I wrote the letter already."

And the angry flowers burn themselves out,
Like the fire on the mountain
Without the water from Markarian to help.
And I wonder where 12 wild horses sleep tonight?

Poems from THE PASSIONATE SHEPHERD TO HIS LOVE AND HER RESPONSES (Somewhere in Time)

The Passionate Shepherd – 1

A telegram to my love—I'm in a time warp:
Reading Neruda's poetry, listening to Joe Cocker,
Looking everywhere for you, not finding you.
Remembering something of your atmosphere,
A lightness *navegando en la espuma*, sailing in the foam.
Nymph, listen to one who can't see anyone but you.
There are church bells to be washed in my kitchen,
A hair tie needs to be removed from my hair,
Someone has to smudge the bed with sage,
Lead me, as if blind, to your council.

His Love Replies – 2

How can I turn away those baskets of flowers?
How can I say good-bye to the love in your eyes?
Looking into your eyes, I travel,
To unknown places of the mind
I blossom under the warmth of your smile.
I open to the welcome in your voice,
Under the sky of your eyes,
I am a flower unfurling its petals.
My whole being turns to you.
But I must step back.
You are a part of my ancient memories,
You are an enchantment,
I must go back.
It could be so easy to step into that world,
Filled with baskets of fragrant flowers.
But I am being called,
Those sweet voices that have filled my heart forever, they are calling me
back ...

His Love Initiates – 3

In my dreams, you come to me naked.
I walk into your arms,
Eyes meet, lips meet.
How could there be so much sweetness in a kiss,
A kiss that travels deep inside, melting me, warming me?
...
A long while ago,
First, I saw your shoulder, and then I saw your thigh.
With a shudder of surprise, I knew I wanted you.

...
And God,
You are my love god,
Don't stop. Don't stop.
Fill me with your love.
Hopelessly, helplessly yours.

The Passionate Shepherd to his Love – 6

Nymph—I've been longing for you all day.
This longing—Rumi equates it with desire for God.
The aspirant who seeks freedom in the Lord, the lady
Herself not unlike a woman,
The one I long for all day.
Oh my! Is there no relief?
If I hold her briefly, will it subside?
If she puts her lips on my head
And sucks it empty, will it subside?
Hush now! She comes. I am agitated.
I am nervous. I am excited!
"It's only me," she says.

The Passionate Shepherd to his Love – 7

With you or without you
Nymph—the secret of my love
Is that when I begin the program,
I play "Please no more,"
And from the first words, "We started a fire,"
I am with you.
Then I move to Manitas de Plata, and
...
As I clap my hands like a gypsy king, the phone rings.
It is you! Arriving extemporaneously at this celebration of you.
O baby, I miss your sweet kisses.
I miss cuddling with my leg between your legs.
I miss feeling your weight on top of me, kissing me, touching me, ...
Feel me! Feel me!
That was the two-backed beast spoken of by the Renaissance poets!
Wasn't it wonderful!
Baby, I miss lying between your legs.
... I'm missing us.

She Replies – 8

She tells him she has never wanted anyone more,
Yet she cannot take him.
She tells him he is the perfect lover,
Yet she cannot be his lover.
She tells him he is beautiful,
Yet they cannot walk in beauty together.
She tells him she will never stop loving him,
And she never will.

The Passionate Shepherd Laments – 9

Nymph—the day I wept when I realized you were the bear I fed in a
dream,
The day I wept when I answered why I'd marry you.
I can imagine never getting tired of sinking into your being.
That day, I imagined you were considering it.
I felt you assimilating the deep question,
And entertaining the earth shaking implications.
It seems one of the Passionate Shepherd's messages is assertiveness
of self.
Since self is God,
And God wants to express herself,
And maybe it would be more fun
To be a flower garden
Than a fire pit?

The Passionate Shepherd – 10

Nymph, to know, when you see me,
The first thing you want to do
Is kiss me and make love to me,
Does so much to relieve this
Formerly battered male's anxiety that
You might change like another I knew
From a loving mate into a raging monster.
That one would have never uttered such words.
When they come from you,
My sweet, mild-mannered and refined one,
I feel so satisfied, so fearless, so open to you,
I can only repeat,
With deep feeling, looking into your eyes,
Take me! I am yours.

The Passionate Shepherd the Next Day – 11

Baby, I got up at 4:15.
I'm driving to the job at 5:15.
I felt your presence at the dawn,
Your lightness of being.
Are you up?
Are we communing in real time?
Or do I just carry your sweet essence with me wherever I go?
...
You are so much with me!
I mean with me.
Thank you,
Love,
The passionate one.

She Answers – 12

O! My dear Shepherd,
I am driving to your home, thoughts of you carrying me forward.
I imagine looking in your eyes, and I see a beautiful place,
Mountains, rivers and flowers, lots of flowers.
Is it heaven?
I feel your arms embracing me,
Your heart, your heart next to mine.
I walk into the calm, sweet air of your home,
A place is carefully set for me.
I'm filled with joy.
I fall on you,
Feeling your warmth, your softness, your hardness.
I want to surrender,
To abandon myself, and I can't.
But still you have captured me forever.
I am your love.

The Passionate Shepherd – 13

O my love—I have phrases and whole pages memorized,
But nothing can be told of love.
You must wait until you and I are living together.
In the conversation we'll have then ... be patient ... then.

When I can't sip from you,
I put my lip on the beautiful glass's lip.
It's getting harder and harder to express the depth of my love.

The Passionate Shepherd – 14

Dear one in love,
That's the reason I am in love with you.
Your feelings are so gentle.
I can sink into your being,
Because as soft as I feel I am,
I feel you are the same.
I feel safe
With you and without you,
...

The Passionate Shepherd – 15

My love, when we're living together
The most fun thing will be to suppress my overflowing exuberance,
(Or do I mean effulgence?) for you,
And be a little shy,
And wait for you to do something—
Think something counts even—
Something like a move toward me,
Seductive, forward, assertive,
Hungry, desirous, appetite on a roll.

Then, to be taken by you, will be most fun.

The passionate shepherd, who had innumerable inner plane
conversations with you,
... And then, when you called,
And after I heard, "Hi, this is your love,"
I replied, Baby, I love you!
And then, before bed, again,
Baby, I love you.
Did you get it?
I got you!

The Passionate Shepherd – 16

Dearest darling, honey, after you leave, you are
Still here.
Your body imprint covers me
From head to toe.
I feel buoyant, bouncing and greedily want to come together
Again with you.
Maybe this separation is
Better.
No work would
Get done.
Children would call,
Demand attention.
So together then, we would
Be apart.
So here I am apart, yet feeling you, desiring you.
Yes, certain now 45 minutes
Since your departure ...
And the longing begins.
I love you.

The Passionate Shepherd – 17

She wants him to move he feels so good.
He knows if he moves, he comes.
He loves her so much, he wants to please.
He knows he feels so good to her,
(But can't think now) she'd like to have him last awhile.
What to do?
He loves her so much, and wants to please.
He moves,
But comes.
Is she happy or not with this short service?
She knows it's not easy to be a man.
She says it's fine.

His Love Comes Back Finally – 18

My dear one,
I feel buoyant, floating in the sea of love,
A sea of your love,
For every time that you have told me you love me,
For every time you have enveloped me in your love,
I love you.
Outside you are beautiful,
But inside there are mountains, and valleys and rivers and forests.
You are a breathtaking landscape that I want to lose myself in,
I will lose myself, but always feel safe there,
Enveloped in your love.

She Answers – 21

Soft night air caresses me,
Wind chime sounds its tone,
You're in my arms, in my arms,
I'm laughing. I'm crying.
I'm there, but I'm not.
You're here, but you're not.
Can I make the bed warm for you?
I'm laughing. I'm crying.
Oh, my love, I love you.

She Answers Again – 22

You told me I was beautiful.
Thank you for unfurling my blossoms
Under the sun of your eyes.
Thank you for welcoming me with eagerness
In your voice every time I called.
I loved the excitement of being the inspiration
For your hardening manhood.
You are looking for someone else's love notes now, so
Farewell my lover!
Thank you for the sweetness.
It was lovely while the magic was there between us.
Hello, my friend!
I offer my heart in friendship,
My arms to hold you,
My self to share with you, laugh with you.
Just give my heart time.
I'll always love you.

The Shepherd Laments – 23

My lover moves away.
I feel helpless.
It would be different if I had moved from her,
But I didn't.
My love for her remains.
She says the magic is gone.
I did not live for the magic. I lived for the love.
Is my expectation of unconditional love too much?
Now my unconditional love for her is tested.
...
I am in denial, knowing
With the depth of love we shared,
It doesn't go away in a minute.
I know you love me.
I am here for you.
I'm not moving.
Move away if you want.
I cannot stop you,
But I am here,
Wanting you,
Loving you, always.

The Passionate Shepherd – 24

My hand is touching you and knowing your womanness.
I am full of the satisfaction of a man blessed by a woman.
This state is holy, blessed. Yes, I said that, really blessed.
I am thanking God for this opportunity, this blessing.
...
Your lover.

The Passionate Shepherd a Month Later – 25

How do I know she's the one?
I think this question requires a poem.
For one who married twice—
And didn't want to marry once—
It took me two marriages
And a lifetime of experiences
To be able to answer this question.

How do I know?
It may be because
Her outside is the same as my inside, or,
Because I would never get tired
Of sinking into her being.
Now do you know?
Or must I say more?

His Love Speaks at Length – 26

O my passionate shepherd, God's gift to this woman, here is a trio. It must be around this time of year that we began. Mi Corazon is tuyo. My heart is yours. Your Love.

No beginning, No Ending

Long ago we recognized each other,
Our feet printing the sand of a beach, as we searched for pink shells,
The surf filling our senses.
Long ago, we climbed the mountains,
Reaching pine scented heights to rest in cool shadows.
Long ago, we rested together.
I heard you whisper softly, "I love you," I felt your hardness say that you loved me.
Long ago, we gave birth to fine sons,
And a daughter too.
We wanted to remain in each other's arms forever,
And we did.

Sketch

Quiet, shy, dark, funny face,
So afraid to speak, so much to say and feel,
Some say, "That's the Shepherd's love."
The Shepherd said hello.
His eyes were windows into a world I wanted to enter.
A passion awoke. A rare flower bloomed within.
He told me I was a hidden treasure.
He recognized me as no one had.
I may be the woman he waited for, or,
I may be just another in a long parade.
But you, my dear Shepherd, you, you fill my heart with your beauty.
Nothing is the same.

Almost Full Moon

Stepping outside on a November night in Tucson,
Cool air, cool moonlight streaming into my exposed heart.

What is that yearning to interlace?
What is my heart searching for?
Souls hanging together,
Union of our Venus parts,
Losing ourselves in each other,
Departure from distractions to escape together.
Don't be afraid.
The moonlight fills my heart.

The Shepherd Answers His Love's Trio – 27

No Beginning. No End Response

Since we've already done kids,
This time we could do something different.
What?

Sketch Answered

"He told me I was a hidden treasure.
He recognized me as no one had.
I may be the woman he waited for, or,
I may be just another in a long parade."

I think the choice is yours, my darling.

Moonlight

"What is my heart searching for?"

It is something to ponder,
The moonlight streaming into an awakened heart.
I love you, baby. Happy Anniversary!

Four Months Pass, and She Speaks – 28

The Inevitability of Good-bye

The first time I told you I had to say good-bye,
You lay on your couch crying, really crying,
Loud sobbing, tears streaming.

You said you never cried over a woman like this before.
I believed you, baby. I still do.

I lay on top of you and told you I wouldn't go.
The second, third, fourth times I tried to say good-bye,
(Because I had too, not because I wanted too)
Your love called me back.
"Don't ever leave me," you murmured in the dark of night,
And feeling you inside me, my heart wide open,
I too whispered, "Don't ever leave me."
You always said,
"You'll have to leave me first."
I always knew you'd be the one to walk away.
And you are walking away, baby, walking away to your destiny.
Your house is stripped, empty,
Waiting for its next incarnation,
For the power of love to breathe life into its walls.
I'm feasting on the scent of creosote.
I'm nourished by the sun.
The wind from the mountain breathes on my skin,
Through my hair,
Reviving me.
...
Good-bye, my passionate, passionate shepherd!

She Remains – 29

The Passionate Shepherd and me,
Joined in flight,
Across the blue skyscape,
Drenched by the sun,
Accompanied by high clouds,
Walking hand in hand,
Through dry brown land,
Touching stone ruins,
This is our land.
Dreaming together,
Of lakes and soft green hills,
Our bellies touching, finding a home
Within each other.

The Passionate Shepherd to His Love – 30

Thank you for signaling an act of preciosity toward this person.
I start to write the poem.
I watched you walk out of the movie in front of me.
Time has no effect upon our love.
I'm jumping now.
Hush, someone comes!

...
...
...
...
...
...
...
...
...
...

...
We have taught each other. We are richer. We are fuller.
We are more alive. We know what true, deep, love is.
Because perhaps—I lack the words here—the woman, a man has waited for his whole life, APPEARED!
And we did the best we could with it.
I'll never stop loving you, baby.

She Responds – 32

You are leaving me.
I'm crying. I'm smiling.
You are leaving me, because you must.
I knew you would leave me one day.
I always did, but I wanted to savor all of you
For as long as I could.
And I'm grateful for the depth and ecstasy of love.
You've opened me to the beauty of love
Between a man and a woman.
I'm so happy and so honored that you
Felt you could never tire of melting into me.
I am not afraid anymore.
You will always be that beautiful man
Who drew me to him with the magnet of his heart,
Pouring the love into me, allowing me to see into the depths
And heights of his soul. Oh, your eyes, my love, your eyes,
I'll always love you.
I'm crying. I'm smiling.
You have a beautiful new woman waiting to embrace you.
...
But always, I'll remember those dreams:
Driving the back roads of New Mexico,
Walking the shores of Lake Atitlan,
Exploring the mysteries of Spain.
It has been beautiful,
All that we have had, all that we never had,
I'm crying. I'm smiling.

She Fulfills the Shepherd's Request – 33

You asked me to write a poem about my love for you.

Afterword

Swimming, late Sunday Afternoon,
I find my love for you surrounding me.
I find it in the innocence of the dusty purple desert flower.
It's there in the pure and elevating clouds of the brilliant desert sky.
It remains solid and unmoving as the craggy Catalina Mountains,
Bathed in gold.
In my love for you, I find God.
I find the inner light of my soul.

THE HEART IS AN OCEAN
from MURSHID (2006)

THE MUSIC FOR THE HEART IS AN OCEAN
by Robert Best

Heart Is An Ocean

The Heart is an Ocean

The heart is an ocean,
And love has no boundaries, no shoreline.

THIS IS IT
(To the Present, 2016)

I Watch the Mockingbird

An old ceramic dog dish
Serves as a watering hole
For the solitary mockingbird
Who lives in the oleanders.

Hey, what is this a bachelor pad?

Look! There's a solitary male pyrrhuloxia
Drinking water out of the old ceramic dog dish.
Male birds without mates stop here,
And join me in my solitary drinking.

My Teeth, an Unfinished Poem

I have loose teeth.
They say it is because
I could never sink my teeth into anything,
no career, no job,
no reputation in town,
not noticeable at church.

"He was very quiet," his neighbor said,
the pornographic movies playing endlessly in his head.

But then again, the TV
told me yesterday
I'd get gum disease from smoking.

Yellow Means Caution

I drive with both hands on the wheel.
I stop a car length behind
The car ahead at red lights,
The result of being rear-ended twice.
Need I say more?

I stop a car length behind
So when I'm rear-ended again
I won't damage the front of my car
From banging into the car ahead.

Oh, did I mention that I jackrabbit
Away from stop signs
So the extra distance ahead
Allows me to step on it?

One can't be too careful
At intersections. Someone may try to
Turn left in front of you
As they come from the opposite direction.

Then there are the adolescent drivers
Who want to pull in
In front of you
When there is insufficient space,
And they make you brake.

Drivers who pull out in front of you
From the side street
And make you brake
I don't like them either.
They make me nervous and cautious.

I drive with both hands on the wheel,
Looking frequently in my rear-view mirror
For someone following too close
And pay attention to hyper-drivers,
Who pull in front of me or follow too close

With insufficient space.

One of them rear-ended me,
And we were both on our way to the bank.
I pulled out to see if I could turn right on red,
And, hurried man, he hit me.

I can manage my anxiety, can you?
Take this advice with both ears
From a driver who drives with both hands,
A green light should be regarded as yellow.

Cat Poems, Continued

You know the reason
I prefer my cat
To a woman is
She lets me caress her furry
Pussy without foreplay.

Eating a pile of kibble
On the tower
She lets me open the furry lips of
Her furry pussy
To try to figure out which is
Her urethra, which her vagina.

Don't get me started
On cat clitorises!

Birthday Poem

In a few days there will be the celebration of my being 73 years old and the body has changed very little in vitality, vigor or health. The mind, on the contrary, continues to grow and to enter into states of consciousness much more universal than personal. Letter to Barkat Ali by Samual L. Lewis, September 23, 1969.

I'm 73 today.
It's been like a play.
That's life I'm talking about.

In fact, I spent my birthday
Erecting the set for Rigoletto,
That's Italian for "the game is rigged if you let it."
In tanto lego questa revista,
In a little while I'm going to buy a magazine,
I said to Brian today at work.
He's always giving me a "Bonjour Mansur,"
And I've been pretty consistently answering him in Spanish.
The Italian today threw him off.

This show business is a funny business,
Working, not working,
I love it.

Bruce Dern introduced me to Stacy Keach
In the front row at the Loft Film Festival
By saying, "We made a movie together."

I dunno.
I'm tired of it.
The set of Rigoletto:
I don't look forward to dismantling the whole thing five days later.
But that's my work.
I'm 73.

I've resolved to work until I'm 80
To outlast my adversaries;
On the other hand, I threw my hat into acting
The other day.

"Please tell me about movie auditions," I petitioned
The film office.
"We will," Shelli Hall answered.

Cherchez la Femme

Cherchez la femme
Is a term much misunderstood.

"Look for the woman,"
It is translated.

The meaning from *Wikipedia*
Suggests from its original use by Alexander Dumas in *The Mohicans of Paris,*

That if there's trouble,
Look to the woman as the cause of it all.

What *cherchez la femme*
Means to me

Is that shape of the hip
Denotes hair on the pussy.

That's why shapeless obese women aren't chosen
To be looked for by me.

Pass the shape test and
Ass assessment enters.

O God! I can picture her on her back
Legs spread,

Nothing there
But a gash

Maybe opened slightly
The Origin de l'universe by Courbet,

A work also mentioned in John Updike's poem,
"Two Cunts in Paris."

O God, it's for this I've been looking?

Yes, take it in.

Yes, this is it.
I look for it.

I Begin a List of Useless Words

I was in the study,
Looking up the word *oligarchy* for the thirty-seventh time.
Billy Collins used it in the poem "Tension" in *Ballistics*.
And suddenly another author
Used the word *feckless* again,
And I reach for the thirty-eighth time
For my ragged copy of Webster's New Collegiate Dictionary.

You must try a mnemonic, I tell myself.
This puzzling word, shortened from effect,
Means ineffectual, weak, worthless.

So why write, as Atul Gawande does,
"—the assisted living home's fecklessness notwithstanding—"?

All I can think of is a fleck of chipped paint on the floor,
Or some dust bunnies in the corner of the old folk's home,
Some deferred maintenance on the screens
Behind the windows with bars that won't open,

When all he means to say is that
They've perverted "assisted" in pursuit of profit,
And called it a "nursing" home,
Even though sometimes there are no nurses,
And no one really there to help mom take care of herself.

Any writer who uses this damn word is worthless,
Their writing weak and ineffectual.
Maybe this poetic rant will help me remember
Never to use the word and to condemn all who do.

I Edit Charles Fort's Poem "The Vagrant Hours"

Each stanza's a month,
Each month's first line mentions a form of poetry (sonnets)
And maybe an emotion (woe).

Comes the month of May and Fort writes:
"Where he erred once let him live twice
As he lived once let him parry twilight."

What hey? "parry twilight"?
That's terrible. It doesn't compute.
Are we sword fighting with dusk here?

I substitute "party tonight."
As he lived once, let him party tonight.
It fits better, don't you agree?

One Day

A poem about the young woman
Who can't be mine,
Because she's too young, and I'm too old.

I've had children, and
She's had none
And she wants some.

One day, a poem about the young woman
Who can't be mine, because nobody
Wants to sit around the house and read all day.

One day, a poem about the life
I live in dreams,
Where I meet a young woman.

I share coffee with her and think
About caressing her pussy,
But don't because another man is present.

One day, I'll wake up and in my email
Will be the answer to the question
I wrote to an old lover:

"After we make love on a rainy day
At a motel in Johnson City,
What will we say to each other?"

On my S-Shaped Spine

Scoliosis is a condition involving an abnormal curvature of the spine. It can be caused by congenital, developmental or degenerative problems.
www.spine-health.com/glossary

A bending board doesn't break, they say.
A coiled spring is a heavy-duty shock absorber.

Scoliosis of the spine sounds bad.
It's listed in the spine health book, like
A problem, or the name of a serious condition
Which needs treatment.

But how do you straighten a crooked spine?
Hang upside down?
Buy a stretching machine?

Or do nothing, because you
Realize a coiled spring is strong, and
A bending board doesn't break.
Doctor, my spine is curved to keep my back from breaking!

Scoliosis is my savior!
Yes, you were caused by a developmental problem,
You curving height shortening friend,
Derived from being a movie grip and carrying
Camera dollies up stairs with three other men, and
Being a stage carpenter who lays
Automated heavy deck sections
One at a time with three other men.

True, I'm shorter now,
but grateful now
for the protection afforded me
by my curving spine.

My spine is curved to keep my back from breaking!

Bird Watching at the Houston International Airport

Here comes one!

It's a woman.
I can tell by her shape.
This one is wearing tights,
Skin-fitting,
Crotch-emphasizing,
Mound of Venus prominent, tights.

I wish portraits of women
Included side by side with her face her vagina.

Let's be clear here.
I would settle for a portrait of her pudendum.
I speak in the vernacular when I say vagina.
The vagina is technically the birth canal.
Feminists call the vulva the vagina, don't they?
The Vagina Monologues refers to all the parts as "vagina," doesn't it?

Let's be explicit here,
Like the victim of child abuse was in Pablo Larrain's Chilean film, *The Club*,
And name all the parts:
There's the clit.
There's the pee hole.
There's the vagina, to name three prominent parts hidden in the crack.

I speak of the crack first glimpsed in toddlers,
Which doesn't get longer or shorter as she grows.
Top to bottom,
It just is,
Starting at the top
And culminating at the bottom,
With the vagina,
Dead center of her body,
So baby gravitates down and out.

This crease in skin is surrounded by lips.
The several lips

Hide the inner parts in some specimens of female anatomy.
That's right,
There are fat lips and thin lips.

That's why I want pictures,
Top and bottom,
Her face and her pussy.

That woman walking by,
She's not exactly the same as the next one!

Then there's the egg,
Dropping every month,
And the blood,
Flowing out,
Unless you fuck her at the right time,
And make baby.

Then the party grows.
Man and woman make baby.
And baby makes three.

Imagining what she looks like down there
Leads to, perhaps, a lifetime commitment!
That's further than I wanted to take this tribute to
"The Origin of the World," according to Gustave Corbet,
Whose painting of a sprawling naked woman called "*L'Origine du Monde*,"
Draws every viewer's eye to her black-haired pussy,
Leaving all the parts mentioned above
To the viewer's imagination.

Acknowledgements

To Himayat John Johnson for collecting the "Journal Poems." The author hates to go back. Without Himayat's loving service to his former teacher, they would have stayed buried.

To Cynthia McIntosh, archivist, secretary, compiler, for selecting poems from the unpublished *Mutu Kubla Anta Mutu,* for transcribing *Mutu* from the author's journals into the manuscript from which this book's selections were derived, and for her inspiring idea to include music.

To Robert Best for so graciously allowing his musical composition for "The Heart is an Ocean," to appear in the book.

To Moineddin Jablonski, of course, for being my bosom buddy in the 1960s, from whence came these psychedelic poems. I honor him further in this book's Dedication to Moineddin and in the Author's Introduction.

To Saadi Shakur Neil Douglas-Klotz for encouraging this project from the get-go, encouragement the author needed to rise to the occasion.

To Sabura Deborah Perry, my loving companion, who collaborates with me and patiently edits and carefully proofreads all of my books. I am so grateful for her discerning eye, working with me through exhaustion and stress. Thank you.

To Jelaluddin Hauke Sturm, a book-making artist from Berlin, whom I've relied on in the production of *Murshid: A Personal Memoir of Life with American Sufi Samuel L. Lewis, Big Tales: All the Stories in the 12 Volumes of The Sufi Message of Hazrat Inayat Khan,* and now *Don't Search, Celebrate! The Collected Poems of Mansur Johnson.* Sufi brother, great soul, I thank you.

Thank you one and all, and for those I've forgotten, my apologies.

About the Author

Mansur Johnson is a writer who lives in Tucson, Arizona, with his cat named Dog.

Photo by Cynthia McIntosh

68184243R00153

Made in the USA
Charleston, SC
02 March 2017